Stress and Old Age

Stress and Old Age

A Case Study of Black Aging and Transplantation Shock

Wilbur H. Watson

Transaction Books
New Brunswick (U.S.A.) and London (U.K.)

Library of Congress Catalog Number: 79:65127
ISBN: 0-87855-296-0 (cloth)
Printed in the United States of America

Library of Congress Cataloging in Publication Data

Watson, Wilbur H.
  Stress and old age.

  Includes index.
  1. Relocation (Housing)—United States—Psychological aspects—Case studies. 2. Afro-American aged—Housing—United States. I. Title.
HD7293.W34   301.5'4   79-65127
ISBN 0-87855-296-0

In Memory of
HOBART C. JACKSON
1916 - 1978

and

for Stephan, Sheryl,
and their peers;
they are
the hope of our future

Contents

List of Tables

List of Figures

Foreword

It is a distinct pleasure to comment on this publication by my friend and colleague, Dr. Wilbur Watson, having to do with *Stress and Old Age—A Case Study of Black Aging and Transplantation Shock.*

First of all, we want to thank and congratulate Dr. Watson for the very comprehensive study he has developed and for the initiative he exercised throughout this project. We are indeed indebted to him. In addition, our deep appreciation is also expressed to the Andrus Foundation of the National Retired Teachers Association and the American Association of Retired Persons for the funding of this important research.

As executive vice president and director of the facility whose residents were "transferred out" or "transplanted," there are several observations related to the process that will perhaps give some additional perspective to why and how it all started.

By all means, it should be pointed out and emphasized that the conditions or criteria responsible for initiating the transplantation procedures were imposed from the outside by the invoking of new federal and state codes and regulations.

When one assesses the plight of the minority elderly (and more particularly that of the black elderly who were involved in this study) with reference to access to good institutional care, it becomes clear that the invoking of new codes and regulations can easily become a very punitive undertaking, unless financial and/or other resources are made available to facilitate compliance with the new standards. To clarify our position further, we do not object to mandating compliance with the standards. But unless resources accompany such mandates, this usually means terminating the facility. In light of the shortages of facilities catering to minorities and the poor, closing these types of facilities results in the further erosion of an already woefully inadequate service in these communities.

Very few minority elderly, on a proportionate basis, reside in nursing homes and homes for the aged. Most of the non-profit, church-related homes tend to serve and give priority to special populations, which do not include minorities. Most proprietary homes do not accept a high proportion of Medicaid recipients and are, in general, too expensive for minorities and the poor to afford. Those minorities who are able to achieve access usually find themselves shunted to county governmental institutions or state mental hospitals. However, most would prefer to have access to those services in their own communities. It is unfortunate that institutions such as Griot House, where an older black person can stay in his or her community and receive needed care and services, are so few in number in the United States.

Fortunately, at Griot House we were able to secure some needed federal and state help to build a replacement facility. Unfortunately, no special funds were made available to cover the high costs associated with the relocation effort. Already victimized by less than a cost reimbursement rate for Medicaid recipients, who constitute ninety-eight percent of the home's occupancy, we found that the additional burden of some $175,000 in relocation costs over a two year period was, to say the least, overwhelming. We are still attempting to recover from that devastating financial setback.

We do feel strongly that the competence, patience, and concern of our staff in working with the relocation effort, the commitment to finding places that embraced our social philosophy and point of view, as well as the assurances we provided that all residents transferred would receive top priority for readmission once our new building was completed, contributed to the residents' sense of acceptance of the move and to their sense of well-being and security in connection with the transfer.

There is a need for further study of similar situations to determine whether there are significant differences between the capacities of black and white elderly in making satisfactory adjustments to changes of this type.

Hobart C. Jackson
Philadelphia, Pennsylvania
November, 1977

Preface

There is growing evidence that family settlement in urban areas, and relocation (as a consequence of model cities, urban renewal, slum clearance, and other kinds of housing and neighborhood development projects), can have serious disruptive effects on families, community organization, and the health of the persons involved. In recent years, a number of studies have focused on the deleterious consequences of the residential relocation of infirm, elderly people. However, most of the published studies in this area have primarily or exclusively addressed the behavior of institutionalized members of white American ethnic groups. By contrast, there have been no careful studies of the effects of forced migration on elderly poor, infirm members of minority groups.

In the study of the effects of residential relocation on elderly people, transplantation shock is a major subtopic. Transplantation shock means any sign of distress expressed by an individual and/or group (for example, by sharp decreases in level of morale), and higher frequencies of illness and death following relocation from an established place of residence to a new setting. The extent to which relocation is forced or voluntary, and the pre-relocation levels of physical and mental health of the target persons are important factors, identified through previous research, that helped to explain variations in personal adjustment to this kind of change in social and spatial environment.

By its focus on signs of post-relocation mortality, psychosocial distress, and coping behavior in two groups of inner-city elderly black people, this study:

1. provides new insight, and helps to fill the informational void created by the lack of research on relocation effects upon the minority elderly
2. provides new insight into distinctions between survivors and nonsurvivors of the distressful effects of relocation, by focusing on various sociological factors not previously examined or given only scant attention

xiii

3. develops policy implications for training direct-care workers and managers of long-term care institutions, who face the prospect of relocating large numbers of racially homogeneous and mixed resident populations, but who have not yet come to grips with the many ramifications associated with the relocation of elderly, infirm, poor people.

Griot House

The term "Griot House" is used as a substitute for the given name of the home where those elderly persons in our study lived before their forced migration. The home was located in the industrial, northeastern United States.

One of our purposes in the use of this assumed name was to protect the real identity of the home and its former elderly inhabitants. Secondly, our specific choice of the name Griot House grew out of our concern that we convey our sense of respect for the black elderly residents whose behavior we studied, and who—in spite of untold suffering of poverty, disease, and social oppression through the last sixty to one hundred years—have nevertheless stood tall and helped to transmit significant ideals to the living and aging black in the United States. The term "Griot" in African and African-American history is used in some of the literature to refer to an older member of a clan who is respected and depended upon for his knowledge of clan history and closely related matters.

The Black Elderly and the
Elderly of Other Minority Groups

In regard to the elderly poor members of *all* minority groups in the United States, there are probably more similarities than differences in the kinds of economic and health care deprivations that influence their everyday lives. As such, it is probably not too far-fetched to assume that the forms of social and psychological adjustments to stress, found among the black aged who we studied, may in many ways represent the minority, elderly poor in general. It is true that differences between ethnic groups—in traditional systems of values, beliefs about old age, and normative codes for the treatment of elderly members—may differentially inhibit the effects of stressors on the elderly members of each group. Nevertheless, to the extent that there are socially determined similarities between minorities that cut across their cultural differences, this case study of Griot House and the forced migration of its elderly residents will probably contain insights that parallel the characteristics of the behavior and life situations of minority elderly in general.

Acknowledgments

There were dozens of people who helped to make this study possible. Among the most important were the former elderly inhabitants of Griot House, who so generously gave time and thought to the many questions raised in our interviews. Equally important was the support and encouragement of the administrators, directors of social service and nursing directors of the homes involved. During the early phases of the study, Hobart C. Jackson, Hyacinth Graham, Izzora Scott, Geneva Hallie, Candice Hitchcock, Suzanne Vargus, Beth Barrett and Myra Fitzsimmons were especially helpful.

After the study was underway, we were fortunate in securing the financial support of the NRTA-AARP Andrus Foundation and Temple University, which in effect made possible the completion of the study. The critical reading of our research proposal and final product, along with methodological suggestions and encouragement—given by Douglass B. Campbell and Frederick J. Ferris of the Andrus Foundation, M. Powell Lawton of the Philadelphia Geriatric Center, Ron Manuel and Ralph Gomes of Howard University, and Aaron Gresson of Boston University—contributed immeasurably to the fruitfulness of the final product.

Efficiency in data collection is indispensable in all research projects. It is especially important and difficult to achieve efficiency in multi-phased, experimentally designed field studies. I was fortunate to have as research assistants on this project Suzanne Vargus, Dorothy Spicer, Beth Barrett, Freida Henderson, Donna Chavers and Harry Shanis, who understood this problem and helped, through their commitment, to make possible the completion of this study on time. Finally, the patience shown by Lynda Ellis and Sharon Geller during the period of our research at Temple University, and the efforts of Camille Hubbard, Cynthia Booze and

Cecelia Heflin, during the final weeks at The National Center on Black Aged, in deciphering and typing from pages of my occasionally hurried writing, helped to produce the readable form of the manuscript that now appears before you.

CHAPTER 1

Social Change, Stress and Coping Behavior

Much has been written about the history and sociology of black Americans in the United States. Such monumental works as Frazier's (1957) revised edition of *The Negro in the United States, The American Dilemma* by Myrdal (1944), and the numerous books and articles by DuBois (Aptheker 1973) are noteworthy. However, while these and other authors have discussed a variety of subtopics in this area, the effects of social change in life situations of older blacks in the sociohistorical context have seldom been isolated for separate analysis. Nor, I hasten to add, is that the aim of this study. Our primary focus is on stress and coping behavior among older blacks under conditions of involuntary residential relocation. References in this study to the history of black aging are intended solely to establish pertinent sociohistorical background factors that help to explain our observations on the coping behavior of older blacks under conditions of stress.

In many of the available social and historical materials, there is general agreement that black elders have traditionally been treated with great respect in their families and other community organizations (Hull 1972, pp. 191, 198; Frazier 1957; Dancey 1977). "Griots" or indigenous oral historians, were especially well respected as repositories of cultural and historical beliefs, legends, and facts. Their ability to recall and articulate their knowledge about former kings, wars, and important events in family or clan history—sometimes many centuries old—was especially well respected (Hull 1972; Haley 1976). Along with today's black academic

1

historians, many unlettered black orators and preachers have helped to maintain the traditional respect for Griots (Boulware 1969, pp. 1-38).

Even under recent conditions of the rapid industrialization in modern West Africa, black elders have continued to be greatly respected for the many useful functions that they perform. For example, in a recent study, Wylie (1971, p. 67) made the following observations:

> One outstanding incident took place in a small, bustling Hausa village in Nigeria. New visitors to this village were conducted to the "Grandfathers Place" where a group of older men sat on rugs in an awning-shaded area near the center of commercial activity. These men were accorded great respect and referred to by all simply as "the grandfathers." This panel of elders served as a kind of advisory group presumably on all matters concerning the village; but apparently most frequently on matters of business, since the village was the center of the Kola nut industry in that area.

Arth (1968, pp. 242-244) has also observed that elderly Ibo of West Africa have enjoyed great reverence in their communities. Ancestoral worship and the belief that elders, through advanced age and generation, are closest to those ancestors, help to contribute to respect for the living elderly. This custom is similar to that of the Chinese, who have traditionally venerated their aged, who, it was believed, were but one step removed from the guardians of the hearth (Watson and Maxwell 1977, p. 46).

Many families and neighborhood organizations in modern America still carry what is sometimes called a "classic African attitude," expressed in the careful attention and respect shown for elders and other members of the kinship group. The respect for elders derives some of its support from West African traditional religions, in which it is believed the spirits of ancestors continue to relate indirectly to the living (Genovese 1974, p. 522; Nobles 1974, p. 12), while old people are viewed as approaching the time when they will have the power to relate directly to ancestral members.

As an extension of the general respect for elders, it has also been traditional for kin and other members of black communities to take part or full-responsibility for elderly members whose infirmities had become so disabling that they could no longer care for themselves (Dancey 1977, pp. 20-24; Watson and Maxwell 1977, pp. 107-115; Genovese 1974, pp. 19-21; Wylie 1971, p. 68). Even when severe disability and economic poverty of the family required placement of the elderly in a long-term care institution, frequent visits by family, friends, and members of the church have been quite common. Over the decades, these kinds of social and psychological supports have helped immeasurably to sustain the disabled black elderly in institutionalized and community settings. However, many older blacks have not been fortunate enough to attract and/or be able to afford these kinds of supports in their later years of life.

What, then, are the consequences for the health and life chances of older blacks when solidary bonds with family, friends, and familiar neighborhoods are broken or torn asunder in their twilight years? And, what are the factors most conducive to positive coping with these kinds of social and environmental changes in the later years of life? These are the major questions to which this study is addressed.

Older Disabled Persons and Social Change:
the Social and Psychological Significances
of Intermediate Groups

The significance of the families, friendship networks, and churches that stand between the individual and society, to facilitate his or her release from hostile and socially oppressive others, is well documented (Staples 1974, p. 3; Nobles 1974; Frazier 1963; 1966; Billingsley 1968). Kinship and religious groups are especially well-known for their importance as buffers that mitigate the potentially deleterious effects of psychological isolation, social oppression, and loneliness of persons in human groups (Nobles 1974; Frazier 1963; Marx 1964; Rubenstein 1971).

The emphases put, in social and historical scholarship, on the significance of intermediate groups as supportive social networks in the sustenance of elderly persons are consistent with the research results that stimulated the writing of this book. For example, we show in Chapters 5, 8 and 9 that sustained close relations with offspring, other relatives, and friends are highly associated with positive adjustment of the elderly to the stressful effects of forced migration. These results also concur with Durkheim's findings in his classic study of *Suicide* (1951), in which he showed that greater solidarity of relations among members of human groups was related to lower incidences of suicide under conditions of rapid social change. Although our study was not focused on suicide, as such, it did address the stressful effects of forced residential migration on the psychological, physiological, and social behavior of elderly persons.

Stress and Distress

As formulated by Dudley and Welke (1977, p. 9), *stress* is an adaptive response in which an individual prepares or adjusts to a threatening situation. In concurrence with Selye (1976), Eisdorfer (1977), and our own findings reported in this study, Dudley and Welke show that the threatening situation or *stressor* does not necessarily portend negative effects in the individual's physiological, psychological or social functioning—but it might.

> Consider the case of two sixty-five year old men who retired from their respective occupations. One, who had a few sources of gratification other than his job, appraises retirement as a threat to his self-esteem and way of life; whereas the other, who derived personal gratification from varied sources such as family, friends and sports, views his retirement as an opportunity to indulge his network interests. The first man may be said to experience retirement as stressful; the second has appraised it as benign, indeed as a pleasurable event. (Glass 1977, pp. 11-12).

In this example, the first man apparently regarded retirement as a source of unpleasant or negative changes in his social and psychological life. Positive adjustment might have been facilitated and/or distress alleviated through pre-retirement counseling aimed at assisting this man to prepare for the loss of his occupational role. Pre-retirement counseling also could have been helpful in cultivating new and useful activities and relationships. For example, through occupational therapy, and a friendship group of retirees he could have transferred his work-related sentiments and/or continued, without complete desolation, the sources of gratification that he had apparently found in his previous occupation.

However, we hasten to add that the factors underlying the different responses of these two retirees, or any group of older persons exposed to a common stimulus such as forced retirement or change in place of residence, may be much more complex than our brief comments suggest. We must be especially vigilant about the many kinds of behavior (such as physiological, psychological and social), that may be triggered by the demand characteristics of any given stressor, and the many different levels of analysis that may be brought to bear on any or all of these behaviors. As noted by Glass (1977, p. 11):

> Primary threat appraisal depends upon two general classes of factors: (1) factors in the stimulus [stressor] and its context, including the imminence of harmful confrontation and, especially, perception of the stimulus as potentially controllable or uncontrollable, (2) factors within the individual, including his intellectual resources, coping strategies, and related personality predispositions. These same factors, along with degree of threat, determine the coping processes used by the individual to reduce or eliminate the anticipated harm.

Recent research on personality correlates of heart disease helps to illustrate the problem and the importance of multiple levels of analysis. In this area of research (Glass 1977; Friedman and Rosenman 1959), some useful distinctions have been drawn between what are called Type A and Type B personalities, and their relationship to the risk of heart disease:

> Type A personalities are highly likely to develop heart disease, while Type B personalities are not. Type A's are driven, aggressive, ambitious, competitive, anxious to get things done; racing with the clock. Type B's are more easygoing, less competitive, not preoccupied with achievement, and unconcerned about time (Dudley and Welke 1977, p. 63).

In this example, it could be argued that the highly competitive and aggressive behavior of the Type A personality would constitute positive coping behavior in the world of work in the United States, where a person may aspire to upward mobility and high achievement in his or her vocation. In fact, persons of Type B may be perceived as maladaptive or negative in coping behavior for highly competitive social environments, in which a high value is placed on Type A personalities as the most conducive to upward mobility. By contrast, given a lifestyle in which persons place a higher value on physical health and longevity rather than on status-climbing, the behavior characteristic of the Type A personality may be perceived as maladaptive through the demonstrated risk of heart disease that is associated with that behavior. Clearly, both personality types are at risk. In the adaptive, aggressive behavior exhibited by Type A in competitive interaction, he or she risks the distressful effects of heart disease at the same time that status-climbing is enhanced. On the other hand, the easygoing, less competitive behavior of Type B persons may be perceived as positive coping in association with the reduced risk of heart disease, but socially maladaptive through the increased risk of low achievement and/or low socioeconomic status in society.

In a sense, both heart disease and low socioeconomic status can be conceived as distressful or maladaptive outcomes of differential success in competitive interaction. However, in social psychological analyses, in which there is an interest in explaining the relative success of older persons in coping physiologically and psychologically with involuntary social change (such as forced residential migration), these factors can also be conceived as stressors.

Stressors

Stressors are factors or forces that make demands upon the individual, in response to which various kinds of adaptive or coping behaviors occur. As we illustrated above, stressors can take many forms. They might be intra-individual (internal) in origin, as in heart disease and the depressant effects of toxins ingested through the consumption of spoiled foods or alcoholic beverages, or they might be extra-individual (external) environmental forces, such as forced or involuntary migration, or the tumultuous effects of ravaging floods or earthquakes. Often there is interaction between external and internal stressors. And, some research, especially in the area of mental health, has shown some of the consequences of their joint influence on human behavior (Lagner and Michael 1963; Hollingshead and Redlich 1958, pp. 163-169). More will be said about the relationships between internal and external stressors and their joint effects on behavior in Part II of this study.

The stressors constituting the major focus of our research are primarily external. Forced residential migration or relocation, and related factors are selected for major attention. Also included in our study will be the effects of low socioeconomic status, the rupturing of relations with old friends and family members through increased residential distance, the loss of visits, and resettlement in predominantly white and unfamiliar housing environments.

The Nature of Forced Residential Migration

Whether voluntary or involuntary, alterations in sociocultural environments, particularly in social relations, mean a period of disruption, albeit temporary, in customary ways of doing things. Choosing a new job, home, or apartment in a new neighborhood, or entering relations with new friends are instances of voluntary change. Eviction from a place of residence and imprisonment on conviction for a penal offense are instances of involuntary change or forced migration.

Whatever its substance, it is probably true in everyday life that social change is never fully volitional or involitional. Rather, it is a combination of "apparently" volitional or involitional forces or inducements, in association with changes in the social context of acting, that determines the kinds, directions and consequences of social change. For example, we may observe that a family has changed its place of residence by moving from one neighborhood to another. We may also note that through childbirth there was a recent addition to the family and, coincidentally, the breadwinners had recently received substantial increases in earnings. We might conclude that the new addition to the family contributed to a sense of crowding and a need for additional living space. On the other hand, the need for release from the inconveniences of crowding and the additional money in the family may have influenced the breadwinners to decide to purchase a new home. Still, there are other factors.

Entering and adjusting to a new place of residence, a new job, church, or friendship group is not made in a sociocultural vacuum. In all likelihood, the prospective immigrant will take into account the presence or absence of settlers who are already established in the new setting, and whether or not he or she will be accepted as a newcomer or will, instead, meet with hostile reaction. Further, the kinds of demands that established settlers will make are also important considerations. These factors and others, in varying degrees, were faced by many of the older blacks in our study who, in some instances, were moved to previously all-white residential settings in which they had no previous acquaintances. Fortunately, for some, they had the sustained support of family, friendly visitors, and small groups of age peers relocated intact to their new places of residence. As suggested in our earlier discussion of intermediate groups, and as we will demonstrate throughout most of this study, these sources of support were immensely important facilitators helping to alleviate the distressful effects of forced residential change to which these black elders were exposed.

Overview of the Book

Overall, this is a study of the stressful effects of forced migration on elderly black people, and their coping behavior following relocation from a long-term care institution. The general setting was the metropolitan area of a major city in the northeastern United States. At the inception of the study, the ages of these elderly blacks ranged from fifty-eight to 102 years. All had lived from three to fifteen years in the home that we will call Griot House—a ninty-eight percent black residential facility. Because state officials had ruled that Griot House was in violation of federal and state life safety codes, two buildings housing a total of 126 people were closed in 1976 for renovation and/or demolition and reconstruction.

About fifty percent of these elderly persons were moved to predominantly white long-term care facilities. Some were moved to other, predominantly black settings, and approximately eight percent moved to private homes with family members or friends.

Whatever the place and nature of their new homes, all experienced varying degrees of disturbance in the ways of life that they had become accustomed to. There were signs of distress associated with the changes in place of residence and the demands or requirements for personal adjustments to their new sociocultural environments. In some instances, the requirements for adjustment to social change were complicated by physical and mental impairments. In combination with social change, the infirmities of body and mind made the process of residential relocation a harrowing experience for some of these seniors. The dynamics and observable effects of their experiences are the central objects of attention in this study.

A Note on the Design of This Study

This research was planned as a quasi-experimental field study with a pre-test, post-test control group design. We focused on two groups of elderly black men and women over a seventeen-month period: Group I had forty-six members and Group II had eighty members, for a total of 126. Baseline data on demographic characteristics, religious group affiliation and participation, friendship patterns and visiting behavior, attitudes toward the relocation process, self-imagery, and a variety of other factors were measured on all members of both groups before their physical relocation. And, among those elderly who were still living afterwards, we repeated these measures at four months, and again, at eight months after relocation. By comparative analyses of scores over time, we aimed to detect changes in social and psychological behavior that would provide insight into the effects of forced residential migration on older blacks, and factors that would help to explain their adaptation or maladaptation to the changes occurring in their life situations.

In addition to detailed study of the 126 blacks in our two original groups, the study was designed to permit comparisons between (1) different groups of blacks who were institutional residents with exposure to involuntary physical relocation, and (2) institutional residents who were not exposed to the relocation process. This much was accomplished.

We had also hoped to collect comparable data on two or more groups of older white persons, of which one group would have been exposed, and one would not have been exposed to the same or similar conditions of relocation that the elderly blacks were exposed to during the same seventeen-month period of this study. These kinds of data would have permitted a more refined analysis of our hunches about ethnic differences in the effects of relocation on older persons. Unfortunately, we were unable to gain access to data on institutionalized white elderly (who were either in preparation for, or in the process of relocation) for purposes of comparative description and analyses. As such, the general scope of our findings may be limited only to other blacks who are similar in physical, social, and psychological characteristics and who are, or may be, exposed to residential relocation under conditions similar to those described in this study. With these limitations in mind, let us proceed.

In the first half of the study, we focus on the social structure and organization of the everyday lives of these black elderly before their forced migration. Secondly, we analyze various signs of distress or maladjustment of the elderly in their anticipation and actual migration or relocation between places of residence, including indicators of physical and psychological illness and death. Chapter 6 focuses specifically on mortality effects. In subsequent chapters of Part II, we develop a detailed study of various social and social psychological correlates of positive adjustment, both during the relocation process and several months after settlement in new places of residence.

The major contributions of this study are: (1) the theoretical framework developed and (2) the hypotheses suggested for further study. Certainly there is no claim that this is a definitive statement on transplantation shock. If, however, careful study of the book provides one or another novel insight for the reader, or stimulates the student of social science to raise new and previously unexamined questions about social change and coping behavior in old age, then the research effort and analyses represented in the book will have served well. For the reader who is eager for an overview of the general conceptual framework and policy implications, it may be advisable to read the summary and conclusions in Chapter 10 before entering the body.

Part I

Social Structure and Social Change in a Sheltered Society of Black Elders

Long-term care institutions can be thought of as small sheltered societies. Most members, after admission, remain in these kinds of domociles—carefully protected and/or concealed from outsiders, with their behavior closely regulated by gatekeepers—until they are transferred to another long-term care setting, an intensive care ward of a general hospital, return to live with offspring or guardians, or die.

Long-term care does not necessarily begin with the assignment of a chronically ill person to a specialized institution. Instead, it begins—or the need for it is established—when a person, in body or mind, becomes host to a chronic disabling illness, accident, or congenital condition that impairs his or her ability to act in socially acceptable ways in everyday life. The onset of a debilitating condition can occur at any time, from birth through senecense, or in any place, from community settings to retirement villages. Similarly, the need for long-term care of an individual, whether elderly or not, can be established by members of a community long before the needy person is aware of it, and is brought to the attention of health professionals and/or admitted to a specialized institution for such care.

The internal order of large, long-term care institutions for the aged (100 beds or more) features aspects of many of the structural characteristics of society at large. This includes surrogate kinship groups, religious activities, aspects of social stratification, economic and political organizations, friendship networks, and other kinds of primary group organizations.

Beginning with a general overview of social stratification in the social structure of Griot House, we will discuss each of these features in turn. As observed in Griot House, we will show that the everyday lives of the black

11

elders in our study were intricately related to various organizational aspects of this sheltered society. Further, we will show that change or relocation in place of residence, whether forced, induced, or voluntary, must take into account processes of social and personal adjustment of the elderly, and not merely the change in housing.

Forced residential relocation, in particular, must be examined broadly as a stressful process that strains and possibly brings about not only radical alterations in the psychological and physiological functioning of the elderly, but changes in the social structures that have direct influences on their well-being, as well. In the process, the stressors associated with relocation may endanger the physical and mental health of the elderly, or life itself.

CHAPTER 2

Social Stratification

It is generally recognized in sociological and anthropological literature that there are no known unstratified societies. By social stratification, we mean the organization of groups and group members by inequalities between them in, for example, income, education, power, prestige, and other dimensions of rank.

In addition to social determinants of rank, there are also rank differences between persons and groups that may be a consequence of age, temperament, physical strength, size, and so on. For example, a person who lives for twenty years of age is ranked older, chronologically, than someone who only lives to age five. These phenomena represent naturally determined variations between characteristics of members of groups that may be differentially valued by them, and subsequently influence the importance assigned to individual status in a social hierarchy. Elderly members of a society, who have sustained gainful employment through learned social skills and efficient performance, may become demoted, or even lose their jobs as a consequence of reaching an age that is socially defined and legally sanctioned as the age of mandatory retirement.

Even in long-term care institutions, such as mental hospitals and homes for the elderly, there is no shortage of evidence of social stratification. Although the criteria may not be identical with the criteria used to rank persons still gainfully employed in the labor force, and who are actively engaged in the larger society, rank differences and differential treatment of persons and groups in long-term care are no less explicit.

In this chapter we will describe and discuss various aspects of stratification in the social organization of long term care. Drawing primarily upon the data arising from our study of Griot House, we will describe characteristics of economic status, educational level, occupational background, physical self-maintenance ability, and the mental status of the residents in the social organization of Griot House before its doors were closed and the residents forced to evacuate in 1976. Then, as we proceed in subsequent chapters to study self-image, the significance of religion, primary groups, and social change, we will build upon the findings described in this chapter to construct an increasingly comprehensive explanation of the social organization and coping behavior of elderly blacks in distress—particularly, but not exclusively, distress associated with residential relocation.[1]

General Characteristics of Inequalities
Among the Elderly in this Study

There were three economic classes of elderly defined by differences in ability to pay the costs of the long-term care received at Griot House. The frequency and percentage distributions are shown in Table 2.1.

TABLE 2.1
Economic Classes of Elderly Blacks Differentiated by
Ability to Pay the Costs of Their Own Long-Term Care

Classes	f_i	%
Fully Private	10	9
Partial Subsistence	88	76
Welfare Only	18	15
	116	100%

If we permitted ourselves the convenience of conventional social science labels, it would appear—in Table 2.1—that members of the "upper" economic class, who account for nine percent in the distribution, were clearly the least numerous in this population. Following in order by frequency were members of the "lower" class, fifteen percent, and finally, there was the "middle" class, constituting seventy-six percent of the total. But, as we will see in the discussion that follows, such an interpretation could be grossly misleading. It is arguable that our sample is overwhelmingly lower-class black, not middle-class in characteristics.

Some of the distressful effects of low socioeconomic class, such as powerlessness to regulate events in everyday life, and feelings of social and psychological distance from ethnically unfamiliar other people, have been most extensively demonstrated in sociological research on psychiatric disorder (Hollingshead and Redlich 1953; 1958; Faris and Dunham 1967; Langner and Michael 1963). One of the most striking and consistent findings shows an inverse relationship between socioeconomic class and the incidence of diagnosed psychiatric disorder: generally stated, the lower the socioeconomic class, the higher the incidence of mental illness. Although research in psychiatric sociology has not been specifically focused on elderly members of the populations studied, the consistent finding of signs of intense distress, in association with low socioeconomic class, helps to highlight the significance of socioeconomic class in studies of stress and old age. Levels of achievement in formal education also help to explain class and status differences in human groups.

Education

In educational attainment, the members of our population ranged from zero to eighteen years. The frequency and percentage distributions shown in Table 2.2 are illustrative. Five years was the modal number of years of education. It should be noted that there were no significant differences between men and women in level of education.

Seventy-nine percent of the 110 elderly reporting had nine years of education or less, and six percent reported no education at all. Considering the entrenched structures of racial discrimination opposing black admissions to public and private schools, and the deep economic poverty of individuals and communities of black Americans during the period between 1880 and 1920, it is remarkable that as many of these black elderly had achieved as many years of education as those reported. Further, considering educational attainment as an indicator of successful acquisition of marketable skills in a highly competitive world of work, the overall low level of education and training helps to explain the high frequency of black elderly who were totally dependent on old age assistance to pay the costs of their long-term care.

Following Billingsley's characterization of the educational and occupational backgrounds of the "working poor and nonworking poor" among members of black families, the great majority of the elderly in our study can be thought of as lower-class black persons:

The working poor families are often headed by unskilled laborers, service workers and domestics. More Negro men work as janitors or porters than in any other specific occupation.

Then, we come . . . to that group on the bottom of the economic ladder who occupy the lowest status in both the general community and the Negro community. These are the *nonworking poor,* that 15 or 20 percent of Negro families headed by members with less than eighth grade education; who are intermittently, if at all, employed, and who have very low levels of job skills. These are families often supported by (other)[2] family (members)[3] and by public welfare. In many respects, though we describe them as part of the lower class, they may be more appropriately referred to as the underclass, for like the majority of the Negro families a hundred years earlier, they are outside and below the formal class structure (Billingsley 1968, pp. 140-141).

Clearly, the Billingsley study was primarily focused on black families, rather than on the peculiar characteristics of elderly blacks. However, a comparison of Tables 2.2, 2.3, and 2.4 with his characterizations of lower-class blacks shows the close parallels between his general observations and the particular characteristics of the elderly in our sample. Fully fifteen percent of our sample was totally dependent on public welfare and family support, seventy-nine percent had ninth grade education or less, and the occupational background of the majority showed a broad representation of unskilled and semi-skilled jobs (see the occupational titles in Tables 2.3, 2.4).

It should be noted that we are discussing rank differences within a group of elderly black people, not the rank or class level of elderly blacks in an age-integrated population. And with the exception of the nine percent fully private paying elderly, and the four percent with post-secondary education, it might even be said that we are discussing class differences between the upper-lower, the middle-lower, and the lower-lower elderly blacks. This conclusion concurs with the implications of Billingsley's (1968) study, and a recent estimate by Jackson (1972, p. 115) about socioeconomic class characteristics of elderly black Americans: "By any national classification, a majority of aged blacks are of lower socioeconomic status, some are of middle and others, although fewer, (are) of upper socioeconomic statuses."

Our analysis of the relationship between economic status and educational background did not show that high education was necessarily associated with high ability to pay the costs of long-term care. In one of our study groups there was a positive but statistically insignificant relationship between education and ability to pay. However, in the other group, the relationship was the opposite. The inconsistencies in the directions of relationships suggested that the variable of educational attainment, alone, was not sufficient to explain the observed variation in ability to pay, or economic status.

TABLE 2.2
Variations in Levels of Educational Attainment*

Years of Education	f_i	%
10-18	1	1
13-15	3	3
10-12	19	17
7-9	20	18
4-6	38	35
1-3	22	20
No Education	7	6
	110	100%

*For 16 persons, we had no information at all on educational attainment.

Occupational Background

Through sociohistorical research, the occupational oppression of black Americans in the world of work has been well-documented (Du Bois 1911, 1969; Logan 1957; Blackwell 1975). An excerpt from an interview with one of the elderly males in our study is illustrative. This eighty-two year old man had thirty years of experience as a craftsman of prostheses in the southern United States. He moved to Philadelphia in 1940, applied for a job in a prosthesis manufacturing shop, and was told, "You have good potential. But, I can't, as one man, give you the opportunity you need because the fellas working under me won't work at all if a black man is hired."

TABLE 2.3
Frequency Distribution of Occupational Titles for
Black Elderly Females in this Study

Occupational Titles

	f_i
Domestics and Kindred Occupations	45
Housewife	14
Housekeeper (Institutional, laundry, Hospital)	8
Seamstress (Sewing Machine Operator, Dressmaker)	7
Nurse (LPN, Home Nurse, Practical Nurse)	6
Cook	5
Hotel Worker (Chamber Maid)	2
Beautician	2
Factory	2
Cafeteria Worker	1
Church Clerk	1
Farm Worker	1
Laborer	1
Laundress	1
Maid (Department Store)	1
Matron	1
Presser	1
Secretary	1
Teacher	1

N = 101

TABLE 2.4
Frequency Distribution of Occupational Titles for
Black Elderly Males in this Study

Occupational Titles	f_i
Maintenance	4
Letter Carrier	3
Elevator Operator	2
Waiter	2
Carpenter	1
Cook	1
Lab (Quality Control Operator Chemical Plant)	1
Mailroom	1
Matron	1
Mechanic	1
Messenger	1
Railroad Worker	1
Self Employed (General Utilities)	1
Trucker	1
Waiter	1

N =   22

In commenting further about his willingness to deny his experience and begin with a position beneath his qualifications, this elderly black man revealed, "I even tried to get in there as a floor sweeper. You know, to kinda bring myself in slowly, gradually, so they could see what I could do. But they even refused to have a colored person in the shop floor workers."

Even though the development of organized labor in the United States has led to improved working conditions, wages, and fringe benefits for many workers, the gains made by black workers, in spite of increasing levels of education, have been significantly fewer and far more gradual, overall, than the gains made by white Americans and other non-black workers (Boggs 1965). Even today it is not unusual to find large numbers of blacks, who earned college credits and/or degrees decades ago, employed as postal clerks, transit, and assembly-line workers. These are jobs for which they were (and still are) clearly overqualified, but which were among the few positions made accessible by less intensive racial discrimination in hiring and firing (Boggs 1965). Given this history of racial discrimination in the United States, the inconsistency in the value of education in explaining the economic status of today's black elderly is not surprising. Nevertheless, it is useful to take a closer look at some of the characteristics of the occupational backgrounds of the elderly persons in our study.

The great majority of the elderly in this study were characterized by unskilled, semi-skilled, and skilled occupational backgrounds. They included one teacher (college graduate), one secretary, one presser, two beauticians, six non-professional nurses, and seven seamstresses. All of these were female. With the exception of the teacher, who could be considered professional, all of these occupations were classified as skilled. Among the male members, only three had jobs that could be classified as skilled: one carpenter, one mechanic, and one trucker.

Overall these findings confirm our earlier hunch that these elderly persons were generally employed in low-skilled, menial jobs as domestic workers and farm laborers. These positions were probably temporary or part-time in many instances, and low-paying as well. There should be no wonder that fourteen percent were totally dependent on public welfare for their subsistence in old age. We will have more to say about this later.

Health Status

Two different rankings of health status were used in this study: (1) physical self-maintenance ability and (2) mental status. A sixteen-item checklist for nurses' ratings of disability was used to determine these rankings. Twelve items of the scale focused on physical self-maintenance and four items pertained to mental status. Generally, there were decreasing levels of physical and mental health status in association with growing old after sixty years of age (G=.15, $p <$ .001, and .21, $p<$.001, n=123 respectively).[4] These findings are consistent with previous research on health status and advancing old age (Lowenthal 1964; Brody et al. 1971).

Economic Poverty, Low Mental Status, and the Role of Impersonal Health Care Bureaucrats Versus Primary Groups in the Relocation Process

Neither level of education nor physical self-maintenance ability were significantly related to the probability that impersonal bureaucrats would intervene in the process of finding new homes and relocating the elderly persons in our study. But economic and mental status were related to this kind of intervention system.

Members of the state relocation team, composed of three nurses and one social worker, the Departments of Social Service and Nursing at Griot House, and family members of the elderly were the principal persons who participated in the relocation process, outside of the initiatives taken by the elderly themselves. In the order named above, these subgroups of participants were conceived on a continuum of affective distance in relations with the elderly, varying from secondary (very impersonal) to primary (very personal) group relations.

The state team was a secondary group with no interest in the elderly, except in implementing their relocation with a minimum of stress. Children and siblings, primary group members with affective and family interests in the elderly, were concerned with relocation as well as minimizing stress. Finally, the nursing and social service staff at Griot House were considered intermediate. As professional direct-care workers, they were, to some extent, impersonal in their relations, but less so than the state team. Through daily interactions, greater familiarity, and expressed concern with family, friends, and the personal needs and general welfare of the elderly, direct-care workers in long-term care can, in some ways, approximate primary group relations with their elderly charges.

We found that: the higher the economic and mental status of the elderly person, the greater the assistance received by him or her from family members and caretakers at Griot House. Conversely, we found that: the lower the status of the elderly in economic resources and mental functioning, the greater the distance separating the agent of relocation from a primary relation with the elderly person. If we generalize, this means that impersonal bureaucratic officials, rather than family and friends, are more likely to be responsible for the relocation of the elderly who are economically poor and mentally infirm.

The most extreme degrees of economic poverty in this study were represented by elderly persons who were fully dependent on old age assistance. In all likelihood, the interests shown and responsibility accepted by the state for the relocation of these persons resulted from the fact that these elderly were economic wards of the state—whose health and welfare was the state's responsibility in the first place. Further, it was unlikely that anyone else would claim or accept responsibility for the economic and logistical costs of planning their relocation.

Lack of economic resources may also help to explain the fact that elderly persons with children were still more likely to be moved by the state relocation team, even though their children lived in the city of Philadelphia. Fully sixty-four percent (n=22) of the elderly who reported children living in Philadelphia were moved by the state team; whereas children and other relatives accounted for the relocation of only thirteen percent. The remaining twenty-three percent of those elderly with children were relocated by staff members of the Departments of Social Service and Nursing at Griot House.

There were several possible explanations for the involvement of family members and others in the relocation process. Clearly, there were primary group bonds. But these were not the only possibilities. The correlation between family involvement and high economic status may have meant that these elderly persons were members of families in which children, siblings of the elderly person, or others had assumed some or all of the responsibility for financing long-term care and planning, as well as the process of residential relocation. As such, the observed family participation in the relocation process may have simply been the continuation of a previously accepted responsibility for overseeing the health care, and general well-being, of the elderly person. Further thoughts on the significance of families and friends will be presented in Chapters 5 and 9. In varying degrees, each chapter is focused on primary groups.

Summary

In this chapter we described various aspects of social stratification among the black elderly in our study, with comparisons between them and black Americans in general. We included in our analyses a discussion of economic, educational, occupational, health-related, and other factors related to social inequalities among black American elderly. Through further analyses of structures of socioeconomic inequality and other factors that we will describe in subsequent chapters, we will seek increasing insight into the influences of social structure and social change on the behavior of elderly black people, and various ways of coping with stress in old age.

Notes

1. Information about each person's ability to pay for his or her long-term care was furnished by the medical records librarian and social service offices of Griot House. We focused on categories of financial means, such as old age assistance, social security, pensions, savings, and earned income by which each person paid, or had paid, the costs of his or her long-term care. None of the elderly persons in our study were employed at the time of the research. Nor did we have information about the dollar values of the other resources named above.

2. This parenthetical term was added for clarification.

3. This term was added for clarification.

4. The statistic "G," or Gamma, is a measure of association between two ordinal level variables. Coefficients of G can range from -1.00 to +1.00. For more detail, see Linton G. Freeman, *Elementary Applied Statistics*. New York: John Wiley and Sons, Inc., 1965.

CHAPTER 3

Self and Society

We have made clear the nature of social stratification and the various influences of inequality on the social organization of long-term care at Griot House. Our major interest, however, is the bearing of social structure, including stratification and change, on the behavior of elderly people. In this chapter, we turn to a closer look at self-imagery, social behavior, and other characteristics of the elderly, themselves. Self is seen as the social psychological link between individual and society.

Self-Image

Self is defined by the individual, as he or she is known to him- or herself, through his/her (1) images and experiences of his/her body, (2) the meanings and evaluations that he/she assigns to self, based on the judgements made by others, and (3) relatively private imagery, including fantasies that he/she assigns to his/her own body and social performances (or roles). Sociologically, extra-individual forces such as changes in the social environment, or crises in groups resulting from the death of a family member, childbirth, or forced retirement are critical and potentially stressful factors in the determination of self-imagery. In what follows, we will focus on the relationships between disability, economic inequality, and attitude toward own aging.

Our setting, as in the previous chapter and the next two, is Griot House and the everyday life of the elderly who lived there. Of particular interest are the relations between the self-images and social behavior of the elderly.

For example, how does an elderly person react and evaluate him- or herself when faced with a state of incontinence? Or, how does the person who was previously active outside or inside Griot House (in performing such tasks as sweeping or cleaning a bedroom, grooming, dressing, or bathing) react to partial paralysis, or some other physically debilitating condition which renders him/her—to some extent—disabled? Does he/she manifest any noticeable shifts in his/her body imagery, self-evaluations, and social conduct?

The list of research questions, which may constitute the foci of a full study of social self, body imagery, and self-evaluation in the social conduct of the aged, can be extended to considerable length. However, we will limit the present study to two major considerations: (1) the relationship between self-image and health status, length of residence, economic status, educational level, social distance, and religion and (2) how the above factors interact to influence individual conduct in social situations.

Age, Physical Ability and Self-Image

At the outset, it should be noted that we found no relationship between chronological age and self-image. This was surprising, in light of the emphasis put in other research (Garvin and Burger 1968; Wax and Thomas 1961) on the youth-oriented character of American society. We had expected that elderly people who, presumably, had incorporated into their own identity the value of youthful appearances, vigor, and so on would show increasingly negative self-imagery in relation to their own aging. We found no such relationship.

The lack of negative influence of chronological aging on self-image may be explained by the elderly person's own expectations of growing old and becoming decreasingly active in physical and social functioning. The following excerpt from an interview with an eighty-seven year old black man included in our study is illustrative:

> I'm wearing the world as a loose garment. About being old, I enjoy life at my age. I look back; I see so many things that were mysteries at one age but they have been revealed by study, years of experience, and seeing how they turned out. I approached life with the idea that I wouldn't always be young. If I live long, it won't worry me. If I would not be able to do what I want, I says well, tomorrow is going to be better; that's natural.

The sentiments about old age expressed by this eighty-seven year old man were also quite prevalent among the elderly black women in this study. The following excerpt from an interview with a seventy-eight year old woman is illustrative:

> They tell me I look young and I feel young. I think I'm an old lady too. If I was up where I could get about, you would think I was young sixteen or something. The way I would be working and doing things like they are around here.

This woman had been a domestic servant most of her working life, and was both accustomed to hard work, and aware of the physical and mental strengths needed to perform well in everyday life. Similarly, as she showed in the interview, she maintained a relatively positive self-image, like many of her elderly peers—in spite of her aging and physical impairment.

When we considered the possible bearing of the inability of the elderly to maintain themselves in eating, dressing, toileting, ambulation, and perform other tasks requiring physical strength, we found that these kinds of disabilities had no important bearing on self-image. This was surprising, considering (1) the presumed low ranking of physical disability on the scale of character ideals in industrialized societies (Watson and Maxwell 1977) and (2) the fact that we demonstrated a significant relationship between advancing age, and decreasing physical self-maintenance ability among the combined groups of elderly in this study (G= $-.15$, n=123, p$<.001$). To some extent, our surprise was diminished when we studied, in more detail, the content of our interview materials. The following excerpts represent a pervasive theme in the interviews with the elderly in our study.

> Look at me. God has blessed me to live three-quarters of a century. I be seventy-eight in October, if I live. Lot of things you have in mind to do, but your body won't allow you; physically, not fit to do it. See!

An older, eighty-eight year old man is more graphic:

> It's (the body is) like an old Ford, an antique; parts worn out; not functioning as it used to, as it should. So many people think tomorrow they're going to have youth again. But I don't expect it and it doesn't distress me. I'm glad that I can still read. I think of gardening. I had a lily brought to me last Sunday and a woman was worrying herself to death about the lily going (dying). That is a perfectly natural thing. I water it, but I expect it to go; and, I'll get it out of sight when blues are gone. The same thing happens to us. It has outlived its usefulness.

The latter old gentleman waxes philosophically about the declining functions of his body and, by analogy, that of a plant. But the point is clear. The absence of illusions about immortality and infinite physical strengths helped to explain the absence of a relationship between declining physical functioning and age-related self-imagery among the elderly in our study.

Length of Residency and Self-Image

Public images of nursing and boarding homes, and other long-term care institutions have generally been negative. Periodic journalistic exposures of the less-than-humane living conditions inside them help to maintain that negative imagery (Goffman 1961; Garvin and Burger 1968). As such, it is not surprising that chronically ill, elderly persons may show some reluctance to seek shelter in homes for the long-term care of the aged—in spite of their own needs for skilled and semi-skilled nursing care. Under these circumstances, it is also not surprising for older persons, on first admission to a home for the elderly, to show negative attitudes toward their own aging.

In our study of one group of elderly persons, with a focus on the relationship between length of residence and self-images before residential change, we found a significant relationship between recent residential change and negative self-image (G= −.33, n=47, p< .01). The apparent improvements in self-image with length of residence and institutionalization showed that, as bad as the conditions may have been when they first moved to Griot House, the residents eventually adjusted, and developed relatively positive attitudes toward their own aging during their subsequent years of residency. As we will show in a later chapter on "Perceived Locus of Control of Environmental Change and Personal Adjustment," recency in change of residence may be generally associated with diminished self-image, felt loneliness and agitation. We will also demonstrate subsequent improvements in these dimensions of morale, in association with an increasing length of residence, the development of new friendships, and familiarity with means of coping with the exigencies of new residential settings.

Economic Status and Self-Image

Up to this point, we have focused primarily on those aspects of the self that pertain to the elderly person's attitudes toward his/her own aging. There are also various aspects of social structure that have important influences on self-image. Among them, economic status was distinctively important in this study.

Economic status was the single factor consistently and significantly related to the self-imagery of the elderly before their forced departure from Griot House. Economic status was defined by the elderly person's ability to pay the full costs of his/her long-term care. We used three categories of economic status that included the following: (1) *welfare only,* or persons who were fully dependent on old age assistance; (2) *partial subsistence,* including persons who were partially sustained through old age assistance, but who were also able to make small contributions of their own to pay the costs of their care; (3) *private funds only,* or persons who were fully able to pay the costs of their own care. As expected, elderly people in the third category were the least numerous; there was a total of six, or eight percent, of the seventy-eight persons from whom data were collected on self-image and the ability to pay.

Generally, we found a weak but statistically significant positive association between high economic status and high self-image (G=.21, p<.01). This finding was consistent with other research showing the significance of the impact of decreases in economic resources upon post-retirement behavior (Atchley 1977). This may also mean, as other research has suggested, that those older persons who are low in economic status and self-image will have greater difficulty coping with stress in daily living than the elderly who manifest neither of these characteristics (Watson 1971; Watson and Maxwell 1977; Sussman 1966).

Sex and Marital Status

There were no significant differences between male and female self-imagery. Proportionally, the bulk of the elderly in this study had relatively low self-images. The following table is illustrative.

TABLE 3.1
Relationship Between Sex and Attitude Toward Own Aging

Self Image	Sex	
	Male	Female
High	79%	79%
Low	21%	21%
N (78)	14	64

Further, we found no relationsip between marital status and self-image. Following Durkheim (1951) and other studies, we had initially thought that married elderly people, who were still living together, would have higher self-images than divorcees, singles, and others. Unfortunately, we had too little data to test this hypothesis.

Education and Self-Image

In only one of our two samples did we find a significant relationship between pre-relocation self-imagery and level of education. We found (in Group II) that: the higher the level of education, the more negative the self-image (G= $-.52$, n=39, p< .001). This finding was puzzling for two reasons. First, although there were no significant differences between the mean levels of education for Groups I and II, we found no significant relationship between level of education and self-image in Group I. We had assumed that variations in level of education would help to explain attitudes of elderly persons toward their own aging and, in particular, their ability to cope with stressful experiences. This assumption was based on previous research by Storandt and others (1975), who reported that elderly persons with high levels of education showed fewer signs of distress, under conditions of social change, than elderly persons with less education. It is clear now that this is a questionable assumption. Although high education may be correlated with positive adjustment to relocation in some groups, our findings show that the value of education in the explanation of self-image is not necessarily applicable to black elderly people, or other groups of elderly who share a common race or ethnic group.

Secondly, level of educational attainment and income are two indicators frequently used by sociologists as measures of differences in socioeconomic status. And, although the association was weak, the analysis of the data for Group II upheld the idea that variations in level of education and income would be positively correlated (G=.18, n=65, p<.01). Furthermore, we found a significant relationship between education and self-image in Group II; however, as noted above, it was a negative rather than a positive association. These differences suggest that there must be other variables, intervening between level of education and self-image, to explain with greater consistency the variations in self-image.

One important variable is occupational history. There is little reason to doubt that socioeconomic oppression and race discrimination have had important influences on the self-imagery of elderly black Americans. Most of the elderly in our study were born and raised between 1880 and 1920. All had lived in the United States during the first three quarters of the twentieth century, when racism was deeply entrenched and explicitly represented in the "separate but equal" insignia spread throughout the nation, especially where blacks and whites mingled.

The exclusion of highly trained black people from the practice of professions and skilled trades, and other forms of racially determined social exclusion have helped to define the social backgrounds of black Americans who entered adulthood before 1954—and the structural backgrounds of many others since then. Given the background of racial discrimination and socioeconomic oppression, it is easy to see how economic status is and has been consistently and significantly related to self-image. It is also easy to see how educational attainment has been less significant, overall, in the explanation of self-image where black Americans were concerned (Jackson 1972, pp. 117-118). Racially-determined social oppression has had the effect of leveling many black people into a caste-like socioeconomic existence, vitiating the prospective significance of education, in so far as achievement is concerned in the world of work.

Self-Image and Social Distance

Implications of attitudes toward racial differences also showed up in the relation between self-image and social distance. In Group II, we found an increasing preference, by blacks, for distance from whites in association with decreasing self-image. Although the relationship was not significant, the distribution of the scores suggested that the more negative a person's attitude was toward own aging, the greater preference there would be for social distance from white people and/or white populated residential settings (G= −.13, n=41). By contrast, there was no relationship between self-image and social distance in Group I.

Before carrying this race-related interpretation of self-image too far, we should acknowledge that the measure of attitude toward own aging that we used was not worded to detect race-related attitudinal images.[1] It was more explicitly focused on attitudes toward old age and the experience of one's own aging. As such, the relationship between self-image and social distance in Group II may not mean that the self-imagery of members in that group was race-related, and thereby linked with the distance scores by the racially focused content of the questions in the latter instrument.[2] In fact, the generally negative, age-related self-imagery among the elderly in this study may be more closely related to general feelings of age related powerlessness, and social exclusion, than to race-related stigma. We will return to these issues in a later chapter on racially segregated and mixed homes for the aged.

Religion and Self-Image

Although the religious factor will be discussed in detail in Chapter 4, some findings pertinent to self-image should be noted here. In our analyses of both groups of the elderly blacks we studied, we found that the more negative the elderly person's attitude toward his/her own aging, the greater the importance that he/she assigned to church activity (G=.48, n=16, p<.05 and .27, n=28, p< .05, respectively). These findings suggest that, whatever the determinants of the negative self-imagery of the black elderly in our study, a significant proportion of them looked to the church and other worldly beliefs, for aid in their attempt to cope with the exigencies of everyday life. Further evidence of the significance of the religious factor was shown in our study of the data on actual church attendance. Although the coefficients of association were not statistically significant, we found tendencies toward increasing church attendance in association with low self-images. Table 3.2, that follows, helps to illustrate the relationship.

TABLE 3.2
Relationship Between Self-Image and Frequency of Church Attendance

	Self-Image	
Frequency of Attendance	Low	High
Often	42%	37%
Occasionally	31%	44%
Never	27%	19%
N (71)	55	16

TABLE 3.3
Acceptance of Relocation and Self-Image

	Accept Relocation	
Self Image	Yes	No
Low	75%	100%
High	25%	
N (53)	48	5

Of the majority of the sixty-five elderly responding, seventy-four percent stated that they were ready to accept their own relocation. However, as illustrated in Table 3.3, the great majority also showed high frequencies of negative self-imagery. As such there is no reason to believe that overt acceptance signifies an internal sense of well-being. In relation to attitudes toward own aging among the black elderly in this study, it clearly does not. Judging by the large number of open-ended interview statements (such as "God's will." and "What must be, must be") suggesting attitudinal fatalism, it seems reasonable to conclude that the black elderly in this study were highly resigned to the overbearing power of the external forces they believed could shape events in their lives. Furthermore, they expressed that resignation externally, through relatively passive behavior and partipation, where possible, in spiritually uplifting activities.

Summary

In this chapter, we showed that levels of self-imagery were generally low among the black elderly at Griot House. We also found that high economic status, or ability to pay the costs of long term care, was the single factor consistently and significantly related to high self-image in both subsamples. In one group, high educational attainment also helped to explain high self-image.

Contrary to our expectations, old age and poor physical health were less important sources of distress than low economic status, in the explanation of poor self-imagery. It was also interesting to find that religiosity and church attendance increased with declining self-image. These findings suggested that high economic status and religiosity will be important sources of strength for the elderly under conditions of stress, such as that generated by involuntary residential relocation.

In the next two chapters we will look more closely at the social organization of life for the black elderly before their removal from Griot House. First, we will examine further the religious factor.

Notes

1. Our measure of "Attitude Toward Own Aging" was a subscale of the PGC Morale Scale that is fully described and illustrated in M. Powell Lawton, "The Philadelphia Geriatric Center Morale Scale: A Revision." *Journal of Gerontology* 30,1 (1975): pp. 85-89.
2. See Emory S. Bogardus. "A Social Distance Scale." *Sociology and Social Research* 17,3 (January-February 1933): pp. 265-271.

CHAPTER 4

The Religious Factor

It has been widely observed that individuals are seldom permitted membership in organized groups—without some degree of training or socialization conducive to behavioral compliance with the prevailing values, beliefs, and norms of the group. Patterns of social and psychological identity, as shown through age, sex, and race-related self-imagery, are some of the consequences of socialization and determinants of social order. It is in the latter sense that we discussed the substance and structure of self as a link between the individual and the surrounding society.

Although there may emerge a clear system of self-imagery in the psychosocial development of a particular individual, there may also be periodic conflicts between one's self-imagery and intentions, and the special interests of significant others. Changes in values and rules for behavior may occur, in societies, with decisive implications for new constraints on individual conduct, even though systems of individual self-imagery and intentionality may not manifest corresponding shifts. Through changes in social structures that portend greater constraint on individual behavior, and that may induce social conflict, there are many potential stressors that may impinge upon and diminish the physiological, psychological, and social functioning of the individual.

Individuals, however, are seldom, if ever, left unanchored in a society. Most are usually integrally related to other persons through membership in one or more subgroups. Through small solidary groups, such as families, friendship cliques, and churches, individuals often find the psychosocial supports needed to help sustain them in times of crises. Let us turn now to a detailed examination of relations among persons in homes for the aged, church groups, family and friendship networks—and how they may function as buffers between disabled elderly persons and potential stressors in their social environment.

Homes for the Elderly as Sheltered Environments

Homes for disabled elderly people, and other long-term care institutions can be thought of as sheltered environments, designed, in part, as places of refuge for persons with developmental, economic, disease- and accident-related decrements in functioning. These decrements, in social and personal functioning, have increasingly called into question their abilities to meet the demands of competitive interaction in society (Townsend 1964; Watson and Maxwell 1977). As such, homes for the elderly can be included in a subset of organizations, along with mental hospitals and homes for the mentally deficient, that function between the larger society and disabled persons, providing sheltered or protected environments for them as they continue to grow, albeit diminished in capacity, in the later years of life.

Although institutions specialized for the long-term care of the elderly are relatively recent forms of sheltered environments, organized religious groups and families are as old as the beginning of written social history. Religious organizations, families, and family surrogates (such as friendship groups) are highly established intermediate groups in most communities. They function as buffers, by providing psychological support and refuge for individuals who seek relief from the stressors associated with daily living in society (Durkheim 1951; Lenski 1963; Kirkpatrick 1963; Watson 1966).

Inside many homes for the aged, as in society-at-large, religious organizations and primary groups (such as family members and friendly visitors) provide additional shelter for the disabled against the uncertainties of everyday life in old age. These kinds of support are especially important in times of crises; for example, when an elderly person is uprooted and placed for the first time in a long-term care institution, or moved to a new place of residence among unfamiliar faces, with little or no choice in the matter.

In this chapter and the next, we will take a close look at church activity, the importance assigned to religion in general, and primary groups in the organization of the social and psychological behavior of black elderly persons. As far as the literature permits, we will describe parallels between our findings and those drawn from research on other groups in and outside long-term care settings, to help determine the generalizations that may extend from our results. In particular, we will be concerned with the physiological, social, and psychological consequences of (1) uprooting and removing a chronically ill person from a known sheltered environment to a less familiar setting and people, and (2) denying the elderly resident of a specialized institution access to participation in religious and primary group activities.

Church Activity

There was, or had been, considerable religious activity among the black elderly who we studied. In fact, according to the records for the total group (126 people), only ten persons, or eight percent, indicated no religious group affiliation. And, for two persons, there was no religious group information of any kind.

The following table shows the frequency distribution by religious group affiliation:

TABLE 4.1
Religious Group Affiliation Among 124 Elderly Black Persons

Religious Group	Number of Affiliates
Baptist	50
Unitarian	20
Methodist	16
A.M.E.	16
Pentecostal	6
Presbyterian	3
Catholic	2
Jehovah's Witness	1
No Affiliation	10
	N = 124

Of the seventy-one elderly persons interviewed, forty-six, or sixty-five percent, reported going to church at least once per month, while thirty-five percent stated that they never, or almost never went to church.

Inside Griot House, there was a chapel. As we expected, the greater proportion of elderly attended services in the chapel. Thirty-nine persons, or seventy-five percent of the fifty-two persons who reported going to church, depended on chapel programs inside Griot House. Eight persons, or fifteen percent, reported attending church services both inside and outside the home. Only ten percent reported going outside the home for church activities.

The location of a chapel inside Griot House was especially strategic for the physically disabled elderly living there. The level of physical self-maintenance was inversely and significantly related to its use (G=.40, n=52, p<.01). While the majority of the elderly in the full population reported dependence on the chapel for religious services, persons rated high in physical disability or low in physical self-maintenance were far more in evidence than other elderly chapel users. High physical self-maintenance was characterized by a resident's ability to dress, feed, toilet him- or herself, and function in daily living with little or no physical assistance from other persons. Table 4.2 is illustrative. Considering the potential difficulties with walking, sitting, and performing other tasks without assistance, and the need for twenty-four hour nursing care that characterized some of the physically impaired elderly, it is not surprising that most would show a preference for services built into the home. These would tax their diminished physical resources less than activities requiring travel outside the home.

We also found that persons rated low in mental status were significantly more likely (than high mental status persons) to make use of chapel services inside Griot House (G=.18, n=52, p<.05). Mental status was determined by nurses' and social workers' ratings of the elderly person's ability to speak coherently, be alert, and recall details about recent and past events. Confusion about personal identity, time, place, and decision-making in everyday life was also rated. Table 3 illustrates the relationship between mental status and distance of the center selected for church activity. It is reasonable to expect that most people entering unobstructed into public places to commingle with other people will be characterized by abilities to (1) articulate at least basic needs through talk, (2) identify themselves and their reason for being there with a minimum of confusion and (3) interact with other people based on the rules established or that then unfold in the situation (Goffman 1963a; Watson 1972). As such, we can conclude that the preference for a sheltered center (like the chapel) for religious activity—by physically and mentally disabled elderly persons—is probably normative among the disabled and their keepers at large, and not

TABLE 4.2
Relationship Between Physical Self-Maintenance Ability
and Dependence on Nearby Versus Distant Centers for Religious Activity

Distance of Church Center from Griot House	Level of Physical Self Maintenance	
	Low	High
Near*	82%	67%
Far**	18%	33%
N (52)	28	24

* Chapel Services
**Outside Services

TABLE 4.3
Relationship Between Mental Status and Dependence on
Nearby Versus Distant Centers for Religious Activity

Distance of Church Center from Griot House	Mental Status	
	Low	High
Near	78%	72%
Far	22%	28%
N (52)	27	25

particular to the elderly in our study nor to elderly people, as such. This kind of preference represents a pattern of behavior that can be observed throughout the age spectrum, whenever individuals sense failing in their own mental and physical character, or that of others, and begin to selectively exclude themselves (or be excluded) from the presence of nondisabled others, lest one becomes a source of stress and social degradation for the other (Wright 1960; Goffman 1961; 1963b; Watson 1972).

In relation to the possible exclusion of the black elderly by others, including their own offspring and other relatives, we found that even among the ambulatory elderly who had children, ninety-two percent still went to church inside Griot House. They were just as likely to go to church alone as in a group, and when they did go in a group, it was most often composed of elderly friends, rather than family members.

Age and Sex in the Organization of Church Activity

Age

The combined age range of the two groups of elderly in our study extended from fifty-eight to 102 years. In both groups we found statistically significant associations between age and church attendance (G=.31, and .31, p<.01, respectively). Generally, the younger the age, the more often the elderly person attended church services. This finding was not surprising, considering the fact that younger members of each sample were also more physically able to participate in activities requiring locomotion (G=.34, n=122, p<.001). As expected, we also found that mental status declined with age (G=.21, n=123, p<.001). Generally, these relationships between age, disability, and church activity confirm previous research on participatory behavior and physical and mental functioning in later life (Rubenstein 1966; Watson 1978).

Sex

There was no statistically significant relationship between sex and church attendance in either group. This is probably related to the fact that we found no differences between men and women in physical self-maintenance, ambulatory abilities, and mental status. Men and women were equally likely to be active or inactive , in so far as church going behavior was concerned. Table 4.5 shows the percentages of church goers in the total group of seventy-one persons from whom we were able to get information. It should be noted that men reported attending church services slightly more often than women.

TABLE 4.4
Relationship Between Age and Physical Self-Maintenance Ability

Physical Self-Maintenance	Age		
	55-70	71-85	86-100
High	75%	68%	53%
Low	25%	32%	47%
N (122)	8	61	53

TABLE 4.5
Percentage Differences in Church Attendance Between Black Elderly Males and Females

Attendance	Sex	
	Males	Females
Frequent	77%	72%
Never	23%	28%
N (71)	13	58

Going to Church Alone and in Groups

A large proportion of the elderly reported going to church alone, rather than in groups. Specifically, forty-seven percent of the forty-nine church-going persons interviewed reported going to church alone, exclusively. Sixteen percent reported that sometimes they went with friends and sometimes alone. Thirty-five percent reported going to church with friends exclusively, and only two percent identified family members, exclusively, as co-participants in church attendance.

The results showed that church-going was primarily individual, and not a group activity among the elderly in this study. Further, when two or more persons were involved, the co-participants were more likely to be friends, rather than family members.

We considered the prospect that the absence of children, and other relatives identified by the elderly, would help to explain their "loner" behavior, and the more frequent co-presence of friends, rather than family members, in church-going activity. However, we found no relationship between having or not having children in Philadelphia, and the frequency with which the elderly attended church alone or in groups. People with children in Philadelphia went to church alone just as often as they did in groups.

Advancing Age and Going to Church in Groups

With advancing age, there was an overall decline in frequency of church attendance. As we have shown, age-related decreases in church attendance could in part be explained by increasing physical disability. As we will show below, the largest single category among the elderly in our study who continued to go to church, in spite of old age, were persons who went alone. Although loners were the modal category in each group, Table 6 shows that with advancing age there was a decreasing tendency to go to church alone and an increasing tendency to go in groups. These age-related increases in group participation, as a vehicle for getting to church, may in part be explained by the disability-related dependency of elders on friends, primarily, and family members, secondarily, to sustain their participation in church activity, in spite of their failing health and physical self-maintenance abilities. Although increasing participation in groups is clearly significant in relation to advancing age, it should be noted (see Table 4.6) that larger proportions of these elderly persons attended church alone in every age category.

TABLE 4.6
Aging and Church Attendance in Groups

Attendance	Range of Age Categories		
	61-70	71-80	81-90
In Group	20%	39%	41%
Alone	80%	61%	59%
N (47)	5	13	29

Both men and women attended church alone more often than they did in groups. However, there were proportionately more men than women who went to church alone. See Table 4.7 for an illustration of this relationship.

It was not at all clear why older, black men attended church alone more often than women. We have already shown that men and women were not significantly different in physical and mental disability. As such, it was not reasonable to conclude that women were more impaired, and therefore went in groups.

TABLE 4.7
Male/Female Church Attendance: Alone and in Groups

Attendance	Sex	
	Male	Female
In Group	11%	43%
Alone	89%	57%
N (58)	9	49

TABLE 4.8
Relationship Between Sex and Agitation Among
Black Elderly Who Attended Church Alone

	Agitation	
Sex	High	Low
Male	14%	35%
Female	86%	65%
N (31)	14	17

When we studied the data for loners in our general population, and examined the relationship between sex and felt anxiety or agitation about life situations in old age, we found that more men than women showed low anxiety. However, the difference was not statistically significant. As suggested by our analysis of sex, felt loneliness, and life dissatisfaction among loners, women may have expressed more agitation because of felt loneliness and abandonment. All were either widowed, divorced, separated, or single. Most did not have children or other family members to turn to in their old age. Perhaps the developmentally intense relation in America between sex-role identities formed through marriage and family networks for women, in contrast to the world of work for men (Parsons 1954), has led women, in their greater positive valence for marriage and family institutions, to higher degrees of felt agitation and uncertainty when their ties to those structures are ruptured. Death of a spouse, divorce, separation, and being uprooted (or anticipating the same) from a place of residence are clearly stressful events and likely determinants of high agitation and life dissatisfaction among women living alone. When we add to the equation such factors as physical disability, placement of the elderly person in a long-term care facility, loss of regular visits from children and siblings, and the death of old family-related friends, there should be little wonder that women would show higher degrees of agitation and felt loneliness in old age.

Nor does the behavior of men who go to church alone permit an easy, straightforward interpretation. While nearly equal numbers of women with high and low agitation, and high and low felt loneliness, went to church alone, only twenty-five percent (n=8) of the men expressed high agitation. However, sixty-two and one half percent expressed feelings of high loneliness and dissatisfaction with their life situations. These are puzzling findings that we will return to for further analyses in subsequent sections of this chapter, and in Part II of this book, where we focus on the post-relocation behavior of these elderly persons.

The Importance of Church to Loners

Among those persons who thought that church attendance was very important, a far greater proportion went alone than went in groups. Table 4.9 is illustrative.

TABLE 4.9
Importance of Church Attendance to Persons
Who Go Alone and in Groups

Importance of Church

Attendance	Important	Somewhat Important	Not Important At All
In Group	33%	40%	50%
Alone	67%	60%	50%
N (42)	30	10	2

We also found, in both samples, that loners reported attending church more often than those elderly who reported attending church in groups. Table 4.10 illustrates the relationship for the combined samples. Although this relationship was not statistically significant, as measured by the chi square test of contingency, it was clear that loners were much more in evidence than group participants. In our search for understanding factors, we turned initially to our findings on alienation and morale.

Alienation, Morale, and Church Attendance

As conceived by Srole (1956), anomia, or social alienation, is a sense of hopelessness, despair, and powerlessness that a person may develop in relation to the society in which he or she lives. Social alienation is

TABLE 4.10
Frequency of Church Attendance by
Persons Who Go Along and in Groups

| | Frequency of Attendance | |
Attendance	Often	Occasionally
In Group	29%	48%
Alone	71%	52%
N (49)	28	21

especially likely under conditions in which people believe that they have little or no influence on decision-making, and the social structure of actual events that determine everyday life.

We reasoned earlier that an increasing sense of social alienation would lead the individual toward greater interests in other-worldly systems of beliefs, and participation in organized religious groups. As such, we expected to find increasing church participation with higher degrees of social alienation. Our findings showed no support for this hypothesis. However, in one subsample, we did find a weak, but positive relationship between morale and high frequencies of church attendance (G=.37, n=42, p<.05). This may be accounted for by an overall low degree of social alienation in this subsample, along with a high value assigned to religion and actual participation in religious activities. Overall, fifty-five percent of the seventy-one elderly from whom we collected measures of social alienation had scores below the median.

If a high valuation of religion is associated with a high return in quality of religious services, or feelings of "spiritual well-being" as suggested by frequent church attendance, then the high degrees of morale may be understood as a consequence of the sense of well-being that grows out of the interdependent and intricate relation between high valuation and participation. In both samples, the strength of the relationship between the value assigned to religion and frequency of actual participation was far greater than what would be expected by chance (G=.71, and .85, respectively).

Low Morale and Loner Behavior in Church Attendance

Following Durkheim (1951), we expected that socially solidary relations and high levels of morale would be significant predictors of positive adjustment to social change. As such, it was important to determine, as precisely as possible, measurable forms of social solidarity and morale.

Frequency of attendance, and the importance assigned to participation in groups (as in church and family reunions) were regarded as indicators of social solidarity. On the other hand, morale, as conceived by Lawton (1975 a and b), was defined by three subscales, each of which was designed to measure one of the following: (1) a person's attitude toward his own aging, (2) felt loneliness and dissatisfaction in old age, and (3) felt agitation.

The elderly attended church alone or in groups. Group participation represented access to, and perhaps a preference for, collective action, and it also increased the likelihood of personal involvement in socially solidary relations. By contrast, going to church alone represented a low access to and/or a low preference for participation in groups as a means of attending church services. In our closing discussion we will explore various concrete and hypothetical relations between group versus loner behavior and morale, and the prospective overall significance of religiosity in human adjustment to social change and stress.

Morale and Church Attendance

We have shown that there was an increasing participation in church activities as age advanced from sixty-one to ninety years. However, we found that there was no significant difference between men and women in frequency of participation in church activities. The latter results were in contrast to the findings reported by Mays and Nicholson (1933) in a study of race- and sex-related differences in frequency of participation. Based on 1926 census data, their study revealed that seventy-three percent of black women, in contrast to forty-six percent of black men, regularly attended church. Only sixty-two percent of white women, and forty-nine percent of white men regularly attended church in the Mays and Nicholson study. In addition to showing that forty percent of all blacks over the age of thirteen never attended church, another study showed that less than half of black men attended church (Fauset 1971, p. 97). While neither Fauset (1971) nor Mays and Nicholson (1933) gave a clear breakdown of age-related variations in church attendance, our data pertain explicitly to black people over fifty-eight years of age. When the data on church attendance from previous studies of younger age groups was compared to the results of our current study of the elderly at Griot House, the following conclusion was suggested: While young black women apparently attended church more often than young black men, there is a decreasing difference between them in church attendance with advancing age.

We also showed in our earlier discussion that elderly black women and men go to church alone more often than they attend with friends or family members. Further, the results showed that men attended church alone proportionately more often than women. Our first hunch was that this finding might mean that men participated less, and/or preferred to participate less in church-going groups than women. It was also thought that the loner behavior of men might represent a greater degree of alienation among them. We did not have the data to test the hypothesis of access and/or preference of men for participation in church-going groups. However, we did have measures of social alienation for both groups. In the test of the latter hypothesis, we found no statistically significant difference between church-going men and women in degrees of social alienation.

We then explored the prospect that the behavior of church-going men might represent a deeper sense of loneliness and life dissatisfaction in old age than found among women. We found that sixty-two and one half percent of the men who went to church alone expressed high loneliness-dissatisfaction, in contrast to fifty-two percent of the women. We also found that men who went to church alone had lower morale scores, overall, than women.

Summary

Clearly, there were a number of important differences and similarities between black elderly men and women—in church attendance, the value assigned to religion, frequency of loner behavior, and morale. Some of these behaviors, like the relation between physical disability and low church attendance, were open to a straightforward interpretation through available theory, and previously demonstrated influences of social psychological and physiological factors on behavior. The interpretation of other findings, like the higher degrees of felt loneliness and life dissatisfaction found among elderly black men in contrast to women, was not so straightforward. This finding was especially puzzling, since it was not explained by felt agitation and uncertainty: Black men showed less agitation than women in old age. However, there was a weak association between life dissatisfaction and anomia. Life dissatisfaction, as a link between anomia and loner behavior of men, may help to explain male-female differences in coping behavior and post-relocation stress.

CHAPTER 5

Primary Groups

Small groups of persons who interact frequently in intimate face-to-face relations are of major importance in the development of stable psychosocial identities, and serve as buffers against the otherwise deleterious effects of crises associated with daily living (Cooley 1962; Shils 1951; Durkheim 1951, 1961; Sampson 1971; Lauer and Handel 1977). Married couples, nuclear and extended family groups, communitarian societies, friendship groups, and indigenous neighborhood self-help groups (such as food cooperatives) are well-known forms of small, relatively intimate mutual support systems.

Collectively, these kinds of mutual support systems can be thought of as primary groups. Members tend to interact more with each other than with outsiders, and know each other on a first name basis. Through frequent intimate interactions, they share information about all aspects of their daily living, including information about family, religion, occupational activity, and relatively personal details about each others lives.

Primary groups are commonly contrasted with other groups whose members are relatively formal, impersonal, and reserved (or "affectively neutral") in relation to each other. Members of groups of the latter type tend to address each other by surnames or other titles of office (such as Mr., president, professor, or doctor). Rather than place a high value on the relationship with another person, individuals in these kinds of groups may deliberately minimize the use of expressions of affection, especially in regard to their feelings about each other. They tend primarily to see each other as officials that are useful instruments for the achievement of a calculated goal. These are sometimes called secondary groups.

49

In this chapter we will focus on families and family surrogates, inside and outside long-term care institutions. We will also study friendship groups and the social and psychological significance of roommates in homes for the aged. Although our principal focus is on primary groups as buffers against the possible deleterious effects of stressful social change, we will also pay attention to the importance of primary groups in the social organization of the everyday life of elderly people.

Social Bonds, Weak Ties, and Isolation

At its inception, there were 104 women and twenty-two men in our study. Their ages ranged from fifty-eight to 102 years. In marital status, the largest single frequency was widowed persons. With the exception of two persons for whom we had no data on marital status, the following table shows the distribution of percentages found for five categories of marital status:

TABLE 5.1
Marital Status of 124 Elderly Black Persons

Marital Status	f_i	%
Widowed	80	64
Single	16	13
Married	12	10
Divorced	9	7
Separated	7	6
	124	100

When we sum up the percentages for all categories, except singles, we see that eighty-seven percent of the persons reporting had been married. However, as a consequence of the death of a spouse, divorce, and separation, only ten percent of the elderly were still married at the inception of our study.

Marital Status and Morale

In general, there was no significant relationship between marital status and morale. Married elderly persons were no more likely to have high morale than those who were widowed, divorced, separated, or single. Nor were there any consistent patterns in the measured relations between marital status and the three subdimensions of morale: felt agitation (or anxiety) in relation to growing old, attitude toward own aging, and loneliness-dissatisfaction.

There were weak correlations showing a likelihood of high degrees of felt agitation among married and widowed persons, in contrast to the divorced, separated, and single. But there was no reason to believe that the measured relationships were any more than what would have been expected by chance. Furthermore, current theory and findings on agitation and primary group relations, albeit on younger age groups, would have predicted the opposite tendency (Dunphy 1972; Sainsbury 1956; Gibbs 1972). Our observations may mean that with increasing age, decreasing physical and mental health, and a higher likelihood of losing a spouse through death or chronic illness, marital unions after age sixty may be decreasingly important as prospective sources of social and psychological support for the physically and mentally healthy survivor. The loss of an affectively close spouse to chronic illness or death is, in all likelihood, a source of considerable grief and agitation, and no doubt portends varying degrees of uncertainty about the future for the surviving spouse. This is especially, but not exclusively, likely in advanced old age, when it is equally likely that other close relatives, friends, and even children, will have also been lost. Our analysis of the data on felt loneliness-dissatisfaction in one of the two subsamples (Group II) in this study suggested support for this interpretation ($x^2=28.98$, df=15, p<.05). Elderly persons who reported being married and widowed were more likely to show high degrees of loneliness and life dissatisfaction than the elderly who were divorced, separated, or single.

Overall, we found no relationship between marital status and loneliness-dissatisfaction. The data did, however, suggest a tendency for married and widowed elderly to report loneliness and life dissatisfaction less frequently than divorced, separated, and single elderly. To determine the basis of this finding, we checked the data on marital status, elderly persons with children, current city in which children were living, and frequency with which the elderly persons had seen their children.

Only six elderly people in Group I, and sixteen in Group II reported having children. Ninety-five percent of those with children were married or had been married. Apparently, only one, or five percent, of the elderly reporting had given birth out of wedlock. Of those elderly who had children, those married and widowed reported in higher frequencies (than their non-married, non-widowed counterparts) that their children lived in Philadelphia. Among persons who had children in Philadelphia, widowed persons were most frequently represented.

What may help to explain the differences in the relationships between marital status and loneliness-dissatisfaction between Groups I and II is the fact that the elderly in Group I reported seeing their children more often than the elderly in Group II. We fully recognize that the size of our samples, Groups I and II, were much too small to draw any firm conclusions. However, the following conclusion seems reasonable: Elderly persons—living in a long-term care facility with children in the same city— who seldom receive visits from those children will show higher degrees of loneliness and life dissatisfaction than peers who are seen more often by their (locally-residing) children. The greater the distance separating children from the place of residence of the elderly person, the lower the expectation of visits, and the lower the effect of non-visiting on loneliness and life dissatisfaction. We will further discuss parent-child relationships in the next section of this chapter. Before we do, however, there is one final observation on marital status.

We found that those elderly persons in our study who were still married were between seventy-six and ninety years of age. Widowed persons were distributed over the full range with the mode (fifty-four percent widowed) between eighty-one and ninety years of age. Persons who were divorced, separated or single were clustered in the younger age categories, with the mode in the seventy-one to eighty-five year range. A full eighty-seven percent of the elderly in our study had been married at one time or another, and only three, or sixteen percent of the eighteen persons over ninty-one years of age, reported single as their marital status.

Aging Parents and Their Offspring

Fifty percent, or twenty-two of the elderly persons responding to family focused interview questions said that they had living children. Ninety-one percent of those with children reported that their children were living in the Philadelphia area at the time of the study. Yet, only fifty-nine percent, or thirteen persons reported seeing their children often. It should be noted that notions of "seeing children often" or "not seeing children often" may have represented partially subjective judgments having more to do with the elderly person's need for intense and frequent interactions with offspring, than with the actual frequency of visits by offspring that could be demonstrated.

Families and Family Surrogates

Earlier, we found through our field interviews that some social workers, nursing personnel, and elderly residents at Griot House regarded each other as close friends. They were not merely co-workers or dependent elderly requiring professional services. We also found that many worker-resident pairs, between whom close ties had developed, often addressed each other by titles of deference and affection (such as "mom," "pop," and "daughter") and similar terms more commonly used in family group relations than in professional-client (or patient) interactions.

Although these qualitative results suggest various aspects of the search or need, of some black elderly and direct-care workers, for close primary group relations, the quantitative data showed that only twenty percent, or nine of the forty-five elderly responding, claimed a favorite worker in the home. However, it should be noted that this low percentage may represent the poor quality of the interview question, rather than the low presence of primary group ties and needs about which we sought information. The hunch that we may have asked the wrong question was reinforced when we rephrased the original question, and asked, "How important is it to have a worker friend in the home?" Through this reformulation, we found that thirty-eight percent of the forty elderly persons who answered assigned considerable importance to having a worker friend in the home. Twenty-five percent thought it was very important, and thirteen percent thought it was somewhat important.

In continuing this line of analysis, we found in our combined samples that the Pennsylvania State Relocation Team was responsible for the relocation of sixty-four percent of the elderly persons who reported having children through blood relations. In decreasing order of responsibility, as indicated by the proportions of elderly persons moved, the departments of Social Service and Nursing at Griot House relocated twenty-three percent of the residents, and the remaining thirteen percent were relocated by their offspring, other relatives, and guardians.

As we suggested in Chapter 2, some offspring may have played only a small role in the relocation process due to lack of economic means. Considering the importance of primary group relations (including friendship) and the clear lack of family participation in the relocation process, the departments of Social Service and Nursing at Griot House, along with the state relocation team, played important parts in providing the psychosocial supports needed by the elderly to help sustain them through this forced process of residential relocation. It is through accessible friendly others, in times of crisis, that new primary groups are often formed which—as shown in many studies of closely knit adolescent peer groups—may become family surrogates over time (Martin and Fitzpatrick 1965).

In further study of family relations, we found that elderly persons with children tended to show less agitation and more positive attitudes toward their own aging than their childless counterparts. Although this relationship was not statistically significant, the observed pattern in the data was consistent with our earlier finding that elderly persons who saw their children often showed higher signs of life satisfaction than those elderly who saw their children infrequently. No doubt, this relationship was partly accounted for by the fact that fully ninety-six percent of the visits received by the elderly (from outside the home) were made by their offspring.

It may seem ironic that elderly persons undergoing the apparent crisis of forced relocation would have high self-images, and high feelings of life satisfaction in relation to their children, in spite of the fact that their children were seldom directly involved in physically assisting them in the relocation process. However, it is quite likely that the elderly had made a cognitive distinction between their children (as significant primary others who were closely related to them in their everyday lives) and the principal agents responsible for their relocation. The latter was clearly the state relocation team, an impersonal force over which the elderly and their offspring had little or no control. Although we did not collect interview data to test this hypothesis, the interpretation is consistent with the fact that the state Department of Health and Welfare had found the buildings (formerly housing the elderly at Griot House) in violation of state life safety codes, and required that they be renovated, or evacuated and reconstructed. As such, it was a matter of fact that the elderly and their families had little choice in the matter of relocation. Given their possible perception of an extra-individual and extra-familial locus of control over the relocation process, it was not surprising that there was a sustained positive relationship between the elders and their offspring, in spite of the intervening presence of the state relocation team.

Visiting Behavior Inside the Home

The interactions between the elderly and their peers were more closely related to their self-imagery and the organization of everyday life in the home than their relations with offspring, other relatives, and friends outside the home. These were not simply symmetrical interchanges. Nor were there differences in the sex, age, economic status, and physical self-maintenance abilities of the recipients of visits. In contrast to the elderly persons who frequently *made visits,* the elderly persons who frequently *received visits* in Griot House had comparatively higher levels of morale and showed higher dispositions to cooperative interaction with others.

Visiting as Gift Giving

A friendly visit received can be thought of as a gift of positive attention (Mauss 1967). The visit is an act, initiated by one person, of seeking a close arrangement with one or more target persons who are, or who then become, the objects of the attention that is given. In so far as the act of visiting is expressive of the intention of the initiator, consummated primarily through the display of positive affect toward the target person, and only secondarily an interchange of the same with the target, then the occasion and content of this kind of interaction takes on the added significance of social inequality in the structure of the relationship (Watson 1975; Durkheim 1915). This seems especially, but not exclusively, likely in relation to persons—such as chronically ill elderly persons, mental patients, and long term prisoners—who may have deep feelings of worthlessness and despair, stemming from their confinement to institutional settings that permit few, if any, visits from significant others on the outside (Ham 1976).

It should be recognized that we harbor no illusions that persons who visit or pay positive affective attention to others do so primarily to meet the affective needs of the other. It has already been established elsewhere (Fromm 1962; Rogers 1961) that people who express affect often do so because of their own deep-seated and unfulfilled needs for positive attention. Some support for this interpretation was found in our study of persons who initiated visits in Group I. Initiators of visits in Group I were significantly higher in felt agitation that Group I receivers of visits ($G= -.23$, $n=27$, $p<.05$), with a tendency toward felt loneliness and life dissatisfaction ($G=.19$, $n=27$, $p<.10$). Consistent with this interpretation of the expression of positive attention is previous theory (Weber 1947; Durkheim 1915) on the degrading effects of low economic status in the structure of society, and our own findings, which showed that initiators of friendly visits were consistently likely to be persons who were low in economic status ($G=.21$, $n=29$, $p<.10$; $G=.15$, $n=41$, $p<.10$).

Further, we found at least partial support in Group II for the hypothesis that persons selected as targets for gift giving were more often than not status equals or superiors, but seldom were they persons perceived as inferiors. In economic status, the persons selected for friendly visits in Group II were more likely to be higher than their visitors in economic status ($G=.76$, $n=20$, $p<.10$), and higher in educational level in Group I ($G=.76$, $n=20$, $p<.001$)

Before continuing with this discussion, we must distinguish conceptually between visits in which the intentions of the initiator are instrumental, rather than expressive. Instrumental acts are those behaviors done to, or by, one person with, or to, another, with the intention of achieving another goal other than the expressive qualities of the interchange itself (Watson 1975; Morris 1964). Medicine passing by a nurse in a hospital, for example, is an instrumentality that has the effect of maintaining or achieving a prescribed medical regimen. In so far as the patient is alert, there may be interaction between him or her and the nurse. But the expression of deference and affect by one to the other is not necessary to the instrumentality of medicine passing. At times, however, there may be "real" or feigned affect by a nurse (in relation to a hostile patient, for example, who refuses to cooperate in a prescribed medical regimen in the absence of expressions of deference by direct-care health professionals).

Self-Image and Life Satisfaction

The overall pattern in our measurements of the relationship between general morale and visiting showed increasing levels of morale with increasing frequencies of visits received in both of our samples (G= -.17, n=25, p<.10; G= -.25, n=39, p<.05). Considering the subdimensions of morale, the attitudes of older persons toward their own aging, and sense of life satisfaction were most highly influenced by visits received from other persons. Although the directions in the relationships were the same in both subsamples, the strength of the relationships was greatest in Group II (G= −.38, n=39, p< .01; G= −.23, n=39, p< .05, Groups II and I respectively).

The Therapeutic Significance of Receiving Friendly Visits

In recent research by Watson (1975), Aguilera (1967), Stanton and Schwartz (1954), and Stotsky (1968), it was reported that interactions initiated with patients, by health professionals and peers, were highly conducive to boosting morale, outlook on life, and cooperative interaction. In relations with persons who had established patterns of emotional depression and tendencies to withdraw from social interaction, these kinds of initiatives were especially and therapeutically significant. In the current study, we found further support for these conclusions. In both subsamples, we found strong relationships between high morale and the receipt of frequent visits from other persons, and high morale and social extroversion, or dispositions to cooperative interaction. In dispositions to cooperative interaction, the responses were especially strong (G= $-.30$, n=26, p<.01; G= $-.33$, n=39, p<.01, Groups I and II respectively). Although the strength of the relationship—between friendly visits received, high morale, and mental status—was somewhat weak, there was a tendency for high levels of mental status to be associated with high frequencies of friendly visits (G= $-.14$, n=26, p<.10; G= $-.21$, n=39, p<.05, Groups I and II respectively).[1]

Roommates

In our combined data on preferences for roommates, persons who showed tendencies toward introversion or withdrawal from social interaction, also showed significantly higher preferences for roommates than persons high in extroversion (X^2=9.33, df=1, p<.01). See Table 5.2.

TABLE 5.2
Introversion/Extroversion and Preference for a Roommate

Disposition to Interaction

Prefer to Share a Room	Low (Introversion)	High (Extroversion)
Yes	80%	42%
No	20%	58%
N	42	45

If persons who are low in mental status are also likely to be introverted, or low in dispositions to social interaction, while friendly visits are directly associated with high morale and improved mental status, then it is reasonable to expect that the selection of a friendly roommate by or for an introverted person will have positive effects on that person's mental health. Further, so far as the expression of introversion is a consequence of previously strained or qualitively poor interpersonal relations, rather than the absence of a need or interest in affectively positive relations, then it is reasonable to expect that those kinds of persons with measurable degrees of introversion will show a preference for a regular and predictable interaction partner, such as a roommate. To facilitate a partial test of this idea, we assumed that a preference to retain a former roommate signified a tolerable relationship and a predictable interaction partner. We found that introverted elderly persons who preferred roommates showed a disproportionate preference to keep or retain the roommate that they had at their former place of residence. (X^2=17.47, df=3, p < .0006).

In other research (Sigerist 1943; Aquilera 1967; Watson 1976; Watson and Maxwell 1977) it had been suggested that systematic social exclusion of the mentally disoriented—from interactions with articulate persons in everyday life—could have the effect, albeit unwitting, of aggravating the mental condition of the disoriented person, or even accelerating his/her further disorientation in mental functioning. Conversely, by sustaining positive interpersonal relations between persons who vary from high to low degrees of mental functioning, the relatively disoriented mentally, whose condition is phychosocial in origin, may be sustained for a longer time at an optimum level of functioning than would be likely under conditions of social exclusion. As such, where socially determined and psychogenic mental disorientation is involved, this would constitute an argument for carefully planned, status-integrated residential settings— with a focus on mental status, in particular—where maintaining mentally healthy, functioning persons is a therapeutic goal.

The Significance of Roommates in the Social Organization of Long-term Care

Just as males went to church alone more often than females (see Chapter 4) they also showed a lower preference for roommates. Whereas only twenty-one percent of the women preferred not to have a roommate, nearly twice as many men (thirty-nine percent) expressed a preference for a private room. These differences between elderly black men and women, in preferences for group participation versus acting alone, may represent differences in biography or lifestyle.

Developmentally, in the socialization of females in the United States there is much more emphasis on the value of nurturing performances, such as child rearing and tension management in interpersonal relations, than there is in the socialization of males. Nurturing behavior usually means commingling, includes periodic physical contact, and helps to cultivate an appreciation of the sense of well-being that can be achieved through occasional involvement in intimate social relations (Jourard 1968; Watson 1972). Furthermore, there is widespread belief that a choice to stand or act along symbolizes strength and independence of decision-making in

TABLE 5.3
Sex Differences in Preference for a Roommate

Prefer to Share a Room	Sex	
	Male	Female
Yes	61%	79%
No	39%	21%
N (70)	13	57

groups. These black men, who had struggled to gain and sustain jobs for most of their lives, in a racially hostile and economically harsh society, may have expressed, in their preferences for freedom from group constraints, a quest for release from patterns of social dominance that have consumed much of their thinking and energies throughout their lives. By contrast, in so far as the women were wives, bore children of their own, or were responsible for rearing the children of another family, they were much more likely (than the men) to have been at the center of nurturing and commingling activities throughout their lives. As we have shown above, some elderly women at Griot House adopted younger women of the nursing and social service staffs as surrogate children and, to some extent, treated them accordingly.

Persons who showed a preference for a roommate also tended to be lonely and low in self-image. That roommate pairing and selection is primarily a psychosocial phenomenon (from the point of view of the elderly inmate) is suggested by the significance of the personal and interpersonal factors discussed above, and the fact that chronological age and physical self-maintenance abilities of residents were in no sense significantly related to the variations in preferences for roommates. Further, age and physical self-maintenance were not significantly related to variations in mental status, dispositions to social interaction, or morale.

Finally, while persons both high and low in economic status wanted roommates, those who were low in economic status tended to prefer to keep the same roommate. By contrast, those higher in economic status showed a preference for change in roommates ($X^2=4.7$, df=2, $p< .10$). In one subsample, persons high in educational level also showed a weak preference for change in roommates. These findings suggested that persons high in economic and educational status may feel more secure about their life situations, and might therefore take more risks than their low status counterparts. Incidentally, these results concur with our earlier findings that introverted persons tended to prefer to keep the same roommate when there was an opportunity for change.

Since a move from one long-term care institution to another almost invariably means that some elderly persons will have to adjust to new roommates, these findings about the differential effects of economic and educational status may also mean that high status elderly will find less stress in new roommate assignments than the low status elderly will. We turn in Part II of this book to a study of some of the physiological, psychological, and social effects of changes in place of residence and social environment on black elderly persons.

Summary

In this chapter we described and discussed several different kinds of primary group relations among black elderly persons and significant others, in relation to long-term care. Primary groups were conceived as small numbers of persons who interact in face-to-face relations more frequently with each other than they do with other people. We also saw that relations between primary group members were commonly expressive, or based on positive affect and mutually supportive behavior.

We focused in particular on elderly-offspring relations, and visiting patterns between them, the psychosocial and therapeutic significance of friendly visitors, and roommates in the everyday life of the elderly residents of Griot House. We showed that primary group relations were significantly related to high levels of general morale, self-imagery, sense of life satisfaction, cooperative interaction, and high mental status. In further analyses, we will determine the extent to which elderly persons, with primary group relations that are sustained in intensity from pre-relocation to post-relocation settings, will have a higher likelihood of withstanding the stress of forced migration than those elderly whose primary group relations are ruptured in the relocation process.

Note

1.   Items 13-16 of the Rapid Disability Rating Scale were used in this study to measure "disposition toward interaction." The inter-professional reliability of this measure (using nurses and social workers ratings) was $r=.71$, $p<.001$.

Part II

Social Change, Social
Conflict and Coping Behavior

> Emigration took these people out of traditional, accustomed environments and replanted them in strange ground, among strangers, where strange manners prevailed. The customary modes of behavior were no longer adequate, for the problems of life were new and different. With old ties snapped, men faced the enormous compulsion of working out new relationships, new meanings to their lives, often under harsh and hostile circumstances (Handlin 1973).

From time to time, all societies are exposed to external and internal forces that sometimes lead to disruptions in the social organization of everyday life, and even change in the structural apparatus of its customary ways of doing things. The effects of earthquakes, floods, and international war are notable examples of external stressors that can have decisive disruptive effects on the organization of a society. Protracted civil strife, (such as racial conflict and urban riots), disease, epidemics, and massive urban renewal programs, although less dramatic, can all have similar effects on small communities and inner-city neighborhoods. Our focus in Part II is on a series of radical changes in the social organization and social structure of Griot House, and the stressful effects of those changes on the lives and psychosocial behavior of its former residents.

Transplantation shock, or the signs of distress observed in association with changes in place of residence, will be a major focus. Changes in the incidence of death, and in psychological and social behavior are also described and analyzed.

The understanding of the social structure of Griot House, a sheltered society before its demise, was believed to be important to an understanding of the signs of distress and coping behavior of its former elderly inhabitants in their new residential settings. It was for this reason that we described in detail the social organization of the home in Part I. We assumed that the manner in which an individual or group responds to a crisis or stressful situation, at any given phase in his or her psychosocial development, will, to some extent, represent behavior learned in his biographical and sociohistorical past (Watson 1969). This does not preclude the influences of structures of contemporary situations and conscious decision-making in responses to crises. It simply argues that the central psychosocial tendencies—the modal or most repetitive patterns in behavior—will have been conditioned and reinforced in the elderly person's coping behaviors long before the crises of the moment.

CHAPTER 6

Residential Change, Stress, and Mortality

Whether voluntary or involuntary, uprooting and relocating individuals and groups from one place of residence to another is a frequently occuring phenomenon in modern industrial societies. However, the social, economic, psychological, biological, and other effects of migration are not well understood, nor evenly distributed among the individuals and groups who migrate. Residential relocation is not necessarily a source of distress, but it may be. Transplantation shock is the manifestation of distress experienced by a person following relocation. It may be expressed by inordinately low levels of morale, high rates of morbidity, declining physical functioning, and mortality. In this chapter and the next three, we will study a variety of changes in behavior under conditions of forced or involuntary migration. We will begin with a focus on changes in mortality rates.

In previous research on relocation effects among elderly people, results have shown a probability of fifteen to thirty-five percent mortality, in any given sample, within the first three to four months after relocation (Blenkner 1967; Lieberman 1961; Marlow 1972). These studies and others (Pastalan 1976) suggest that those elderly persons least likely to survive uprooting and relocation are those ranked low in mental status, physical self-maintenance ability, and who are involuntarily removed from their place of residence. Along with health differences, mental status, and self-maintenance abilities, the increased mortality rates show the need for careful research on age, sex, pre-relocation signs of depression, felt support from family and friends, and other factors that may help to distinguish survivors from non-survivors following relocation.

Death Takes a Holiday

In contrast to the sharp increases in rates of mortality predicted by other studies, the two groups of elderly black people in our study showed post-relocation mortality rates of six percent and three percent, respectively, in the first four months following transplantation. In Group 1, composed of forty-six people, we found two percent mortality in the first month following relocation. And, within the next three months, there were two additional deaths, or four percent, for a total of six percent of the original sample within the first four months following relocation. These percentages are significantly lower than the fifteen to thirty-five percent rate reported in previous research.

Even more striking were the findings for the second sample, or Group II. In this sample of seventy-four elderly blacks, there were no reported mortalities in the first month after relocation, and only three percent during the next three months.[1] These findings were indeed puzzling, considering the generalizations that have been made on the basis of other research on relocation effects.

Further, a careful study of Figure 6.1 shows that, with the beginning of the relocation of members of Group I in May of 1976, there was a cessation of mortalities in that group through the removal of the last member in August of 1976.

During the first month following the complete relocation of Group II, there were no deaths. Further, in contrast to Group I, only three percent of the members of Group II died during the first four months following relocation (see Figure 6.2). During the next several months (following the four month critical period), mortality rates for each group returned to the levels observed during the two years before relocation (see Figures 6.2 and 6.3).

Figure 6.3 and the appendix to this chapter show that between 1974 and 1976 the yearly death rate for Group I (up to the beginning of the process of physical relocation) ranged between seventeen and twenty-one percent. In Group II, the death rate ranged from twenty-three to twenty-nine percent for the same period. If we then look at the data for Figure 6.2, and project the incidence of death in Groups I and II for the twelve month period immediately following the dates that marked the end of the physical relocation of each group, the yearly rates will be sixteen percent and twenty-three percent, respectively. These percentages fall at the lower ends of the ranges of pre-relocation, yearly mortality rates for each group. However, when we compared the rates between the year after and the year immediately preceding relocation, we found that the projected rate for

FIGURE 6.1
Incidence of Pre-Relocation Mortality in 1976 in Groups I and II

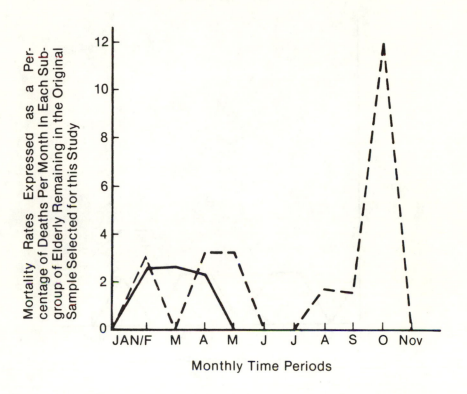

Group   1 ———————— , n = 46, at origin.
Beginning of relocation: May, 1976.
Relocation was complete, August
31, 1976.

Group   2 — — — — — , n = 80, at origin.
Beginning of relocation: July, 1976.
Relocation was complete,
November 24, 1976.

FIGURE 6.2
Incidence of Post-Relocation Mortality in Groups I and II

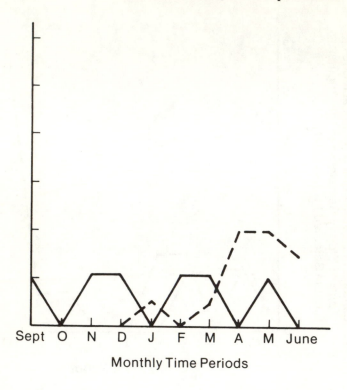

Monthly Time Periods

Group   1 —————————— , n = 46, at origin.

Group   2 — — — — — — , n = 74, at origin
(There were 6 deaths in this group
before the completion of the
process of relocation).

Group II in 1977-78, twenty-three percent, was identical to its rate for
1976, and the projection for Group I, sixteen percent, was only slightly
lower than its yearly rate in 1976. This means that with the exception of the
decline in the incidence of death during the period of physical relocation of
each group, there were essentially no changes in the incidence of death in
either group (see the appendix to this chapter for a description of the
procedure by which the yearly rates were found).

FIGURE 6.3
**Change in Percentages of Deaths in Relation to the
Average Number of Residents Living in Two Groups of
Elderly Black Persons over a Three Year Period**

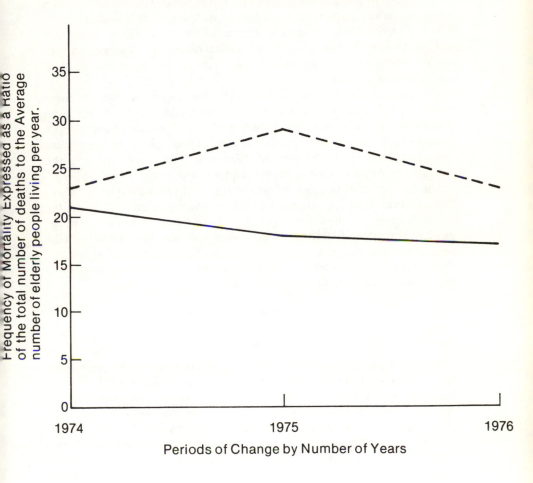

Legend: Group I. ————————

Group II. — — — — — —

In September, immediately following completion of the physical relocation of the last member of Group I, the incidence of new deaths resumed. It appeared that death took a holiday during the process of physically relocating Group I.

When Group I was compared to its control, which was not undergoing relocation at the same time, our findings were identical: The association between physical relocation and decline in the incidence of death was upheld. During the period of the relocation of Group I, the incidence of death in the control group was relatively consistent, about one and two tenths percent per month.

Then, in July and August, when the administrators began to focus direct attention on Group II, the control for Group I, and to actually begin the process of physically moving members of Group II, erratic changes began to occur in the incidence of death. First, there was a sharp decline to zero mortalities during the months of June and July, followed by small increases in August and September, and a sharp increase in October.[2]

The relocation of members of Group II got off to a slow start in July of 1976. Eleven members were moved between the beginning of July and the end of August. As shown in Figure 6.1, there was a slight decline in the incidence of mortality during the months of June and July. Then, with the increased tempo of the relocation process, marked by the removal of forty-three persons in Semptember and October, there was a sharp increase in the incidence of mortality in Group II.

The Search for Insight

Stress in Anticipation of Relocation

First, it should be noted—as we pointed out above—that there were higher pre-relocation instances of mortality in Group II during the months immediately preceding evacuation than there were during the first four months after relocation. This may mean that the elderly members of Group II experienced more fatal distress in anticipation of relocation than they experienced during and after the actual process of relocation (Death 1975; Bourestom and Tars 1974). These lower instances of post-relocation mortality may also mean, as we will show in the next three chapters, that the members of Group II, like Group I, may have made highly positive social, psychological, and physiological adjustments to their new homes during the first four months following relocation and, as a consequence, the incidence of death decreased.

Ruptured Social Ties, Depression and Mortality in the Older Woman

Although women represented only eighty-four percent, or 101 of the 120 elderly blacks surviving immediately following their relocation, they accounted for 100 per cent of the eighteen deaths that occurred during the seven to ten months following the complete relocation of Groups I and II. What follows is a discussion of various ideas and literature that might, through further research, help to shed insight into this puzzling finding.

In a recent study of "Depression in Middle Aged Women," Pauline Bart (1968) reported the following finding about the effects of anticipated loss or diminution of a previously positive relationship with another person. Women who were "over-protective" or "over-involved" in relationships with, for example, children, showed more signs of depression than uninvolved women, in anticipation of losing the maternal role through the marriage of a child. Bart (1968, p. 3) also made the following observation:

> Since mental health is dependent on a positive self-concept, it is therefore dependent on the roles available to the individual. Women whose identity, whose sense of self, is derived mainly from their role as mothers rather than their role as wives; women whose "significant others" are limited to their children, are in a difficult situation when their children leave and former patterns of social interaction between them are disrupted. These women's self-conceptions must change. Some (however) have personalities too rigid to enable them to make the change.

Although we do not have in this study a set of data conducive to testing all of Bart's (1968) ideas, the data available are suggestive. First, it should be noted that our findings on marital status and self-image, as discussed in Chapters 5 and 9, lend support to Bart's observation that in some women, the sense of self is more closely tied to their roles as mothers than their roles as wives. We found that women who had children, and who received frequent visits from them, had significantly higher self-images than those who did not. However, being or not being married had no significant effect on self-image.

Secondly, as we also showed in Chapter 5, many of these women had developed kin-like relations with selected members of the social service and nursing staffs at Griot House; many staff members had been "adopted" as surrogate daughters and sons. With relocation, these established relations were strained, and in many instances broken. Many of the former residents of Griot House were moved to new homes either outside the city or several miles from Griot House. This made travel difficult for surrogate kin and "real" kin, and frequent visits unlikely. The facts of (1) ruptured relations with kin and kin-like others, (2) change to new and unfamiliar neighborhoods and residential settings, (3) decreasing visits from kin and close friends, and (4) infirmities of body and mind— may have helped to account for the fact that all of the post-relocation deaths (n=18) were among female elderly persons. Furthermore, eighty-nine percent of those who died had been moved to predominantly white residential settings at considerable geographic distances from Griot House. Because their social and private identities are more closely tied to the structures of family, neighborhood, and nurturing roles, women are likely to find these kinds of changes more traumatic than men (Bart 1968, pp. 4,9; Lowenthal 1975). By contrast, men are more likely than women to show high sensitivity to loss of occupational role and retirement (Institute óf Gerontology 1975; Parsons 1954; Eisdorfer 1977, pp. 35-36).

Bart's hypotheses about the negative influences of these kinds of disruptions on the psychological functioning of women is further supported in the results of our study of the differences between levels of self-image, felt loneliness, and self-percieved change for female survivors and nonsurvivors. Table 6.1 is illustrative. These data show that those women who died showed significant increases in their feelings of loneliness and life dissatisfaction, as well as low dispositions to interact with other people. Although the statistics were not significant, Table 6.1 also shows that the women who died had markedly lower self-images, and perceived much more negative change, than survivors in their life situations. It seems clear from these findings that ruptured social relations that previously buttressed sex role identity were important determinants of maladjustment under conditions of rapid social change.

The hypotheses of Involuntary Relocation

The scanty literature on transplantation shock offered little help in our attempt to explain the findings of mortality that grew out of this study. Involuntary relocation, a variable emphasized in some research (Blenker 1967; Lieberman 1961; Lawton and Yaffe 1970) was naturalistically built into the design of the research. On the surface, neither Group I nor II had a choice in whether or not they would be relocated. Yet, as we have shown, the absence of choice did not lead to sharp increases in the mortality rate.

It is conceivable that the absence of social participation, by the elderly, with the administrators, in the decision-making processes that led to the evacuation of Griot House, did not necessarily preclude or deny the elderly a personal or private sense of participation and choice. Through the "Town Meetings" of residents at Griot House, and the deeply religious beliefs—held by many—in other worldly determinants of the events in their everyday lives, many of these elderly persons may have felt much more engaged in than alienated from the decision of the administrators of Griot House to evacuate the premises.

For example, sixty residents were asked about their readiness for relocation and acceptance of the decisions made by the administrators. Forty-nine, or seventy-three percent, said that they were ready to accept relocation, eight percent said they were not ready, and nineteen percent

TABLE 6.1

Behavioral Differences Between Surviving (n=53) and Nonsurviving Females (n=14) Four Months After Relocation. All Deaths Occurred by or Before the Eighth Month Following Relocation

Behavioral Characteristics		Survivors	Nonsurvivors	t value	2-Tail Prob.
Loneliness–Life Dissatisfaction	Mean SD	3.3 1.2	2.3 .74	-2.85	.006*
Disposition to Social Interaction	Mean SD	3.2 .86	2.6 1.2	-2.51	.014*
Attitude Toward Own Aging	Mean SD	1.9 1.7	1.2 1.2	-1.41	.164
Perceived Change in Life Situation	Mean SD	4.1 .80	3.8 .70	-1.35	.180

*These differences between the means for surviving and nonsurviving females are much greater than what would be expected by chance.

said they were uncertain. There were too few cases to permit statistical comparisons between Groups I and II, males and females, or other variables whose cross-tabulations might have shed some insight into the factors determining the differences between these attitudes. However, it is worth noting that the majority of the elderly who were asked this question answered in the affirmative, even though relocation was clearly no choice of their own.

The Survival Value of Town Meetings and Religiosity

Town meetings were weekly gatherings of articulate elderly residents of Griot House, held under the supervision of the Department of Social Services. The elderly members used these meetings to openly discuss their feelings, likes, and dislikes about events taking place at Griot House— including housing relocation—and to recommend to the administrators ways in which the home could be improved. Since this was a representative assembly, with participants selected from each floor of the home, both the representatives and their coherent contituents could have felt considerably involved in helping to shape their own relocation from Griot House. Secondly, since the administrator of the home had announced that the relocation of some residents was temporary, and that those who wished could return when the new facility was complete, many of the elderly may have felt much less uprooted, and less denial of participation in the closing and reconstruction of Griot House than would have been the case, otherwise.

Third, as we will show in Chapter 8, high religiosity—or the importance assigned to religious beliefs and practices—was one of the best predictors of positive post-relocation adjustment. The highly religious elderly in this study may have believed that their removal from Griot House was an expression of the will of their God, not merely a decision of the state and/or the administrators of the home. As a consequence, they may have found the process of relocation much less disturbing and less objectionable than persons who were less religiously devoted. To further this line of reasoning, the affirmative answers to the question about readiness for relocation (reported above) may have been surface expressions of a deep— but unexpressed—religious commitment to follow the will of their God, a part of which was manifest in the decision to relocate. Although speculative, this interpretation concurs with our findings in Chapter 8, which show that following relocation, the elderly who were low in religiosity showed more signs of maladjustment than the high religiosity elderly. We will have more to say about this in Chapter 8.

Primary Group Involvement in the
Mitigation of Relocation Stress

Contrary to our own expectations, and those of most of the nursing home administrators we interviewed, we found that all of the post-relocation deaths, within the first four months following relocation, occurred among persons for whom the state relocation team was responsible. Of course, it could be argued that the number of deaths was so small (n=5), that the difference between the state group and the zero frequency for all other elderly could be accounted for by chance. However, considering the emphasis that was given to the potentially positive effects of the state relocation team as a stress reducing agent, these data, however small, cannot be ignored.

It was worth noting that all of the elderly survivors in the first four months were either moved through their own initiatives, by family members, or by social service and nursing personnel at Griot House. In so far as differing degrees of involuntary participation were concerned, persons who were moved by family, friends, or on their own initiative, probably felt much less alienation from decision-making, and experienced less distress during their relocation than persons who were moved by members of the state relocation team. In general, this suggests that the incidence of death (and other signs of post-relocation distress) in future relocation projects will probably be much greater among persons moved by impersonal bureaucrats, such as members of state relocation teams. In contrast, the incidence of death should be less frequent among those elderly who are moved through their own initiatives, or through the efforts of persons who will have had primary relations with them, such as family members or friends.

Further, high rates of survival, and positive psychological and social adjustment in a group of elderly people undergoing relocation, can be a function of the maintenance of established positive relationships between subgroups of friends and/or roommates who are moved intact. This explanation follows the research on suicide done by Emile Durkheim some eighty years ago. Durkheim found that low suicide rates, in any given society or within a stratum of society, could in part be explained by socially solidary relations which effectively suppress the incidence of anxiety, especially in relation to rapid patterns of mobility within groups whose members might otherwise have had a high rate of suicide. This means that the maintenance of social solidarity within a group can function as a buffer between any given member of the group and the incidence or likelihood of stress that might be expressed through suicide, depression or other signs of maladjustment under conditions of rapid or radical social change. Although we had too few instances of mortality to test this hypothesis, we did have several measures of psychological change that permitted systematic analysis. The results of those tests were generally consistent with our Durkheimian hypotheses, and are discussed in Chapters 7 and 9.

Physical Self-maintenance, Mental Status, and Alienation

In the preceding section, it was pointed out that all of the post-relocation deaths in the first four months occurred in elderly persons for whom the state relocation team was responsible. It was also pointed out that those deaths might have been related to the relative ineffectiveness of the members of the state team in reducing the shocking effects of relocation.

We have already noted that the relationship between state team intervention and the incidence of death may have been coincidental. The relationship may be explained by the fact that all of the nine persons who died during the first five months, including the five moved by the state team following relocation, were significantly lower than survivors in physical self-maintenance abilities, mental status, and disposition to interaction. Table 6.2 is illustrative.

We showed in Chapters 2 and 5 that elderly persons, for whom the state team was responsible, were the lowest in economic status and least likely to have someone else, like family members, to intervene on their behalf. We also found that the elderly persons who were lowest in economic status also included a disproportionate number of the severely impaired members in our study.

The findings in Table 6.2, that differentiate survivors from nonsurvivors by physical self-maintenance abilities and mental status, were consistent with the results of previous research (Blenkner 1967; Lieberman 1961; Marlowe 1972; Pastalan 1976; Storandt, Wittels, and Botwinick 1975; Lawton and Yaffe 1970). However, there was no significant difference between the mean anomia scores for survivors and nonsurvivors.

As shown in Table 6.2, dispositions to interaction helped to differentiate survivors from nonsurvivors during the first five months following relocation. As you recall from our discussion of primary groups in Chapter 5, disposition to interaction was defined by the extent to which a person was extroverted (outgoing in human relations), or introverted (withdrawing in response to the presence of other persons). Our findings showed that significantly more persons died who were introverted or low in disposition to interaction—under conditions of forced migration.

TABLE 6.2

Behavioral Differences Between Survivors (n=111) Versus Nonsurvivors (n=9) Five Months After Forced Migration from Griot House

Behavioral Characteristics		Survi- vors	Nonsur- vivors	t value	2-Tail Prob.
Physical Self-Maintenance Ability	Mean	29.0	25.4	-2.32	.022*
	SD	4.4	4.7		
Mental Status	Mean	8.6	6.2	-3.24	.002*
	SD	2.2	2.2		
Disposition to Inter- action	Mean	8.5	6.9	-2.87	.005*
	SD	1.6	1.8		

*These t-values represent differences between the means for survivors and nonsur-vivors that are much greater than what would be expected by chance.

Summary

In this chapter, we have reported our findings and interpretations of data on rates of post-relocation mortality in the two groups of elderly black people who were forced to leave Griot House in 1976. Both groups had lower proportions of post-relocation mortalities than the proportions hypothesized on the basis of previous research focusing on other ethnic groups.

There was evidence that the anticipation of relocation may have been more traumatic than relocation itself. In contrast to findings of previous research, we found a decrease, rather than an increase, in the incidence of death during both the process of relocation itself, and (in one group) the first four months after relocation. We found no clear explanation for these particular changes, but we did identify a number of factors that helped to differentiate survivors from nonsurvivors in this study.

All of the post-relocation deaths occurred among females in this study. The differential disruption of lifestyles, severe role losses, and depression were discussed as factors that help to explain the disproportionate incidence of death among older women under conditions of radical social change. In addition, when compared to women who survived, those who died reported significantly more loneliness and life dissatisfaction, and showed greater withdrawal from social interaction during the weeks or months immediately preceding their deaths.

When we compared all deaths to all survivors, regardless of sex, during the first four months following relocation, those persons who died were significantly lower than survivors in physical self-maintenance ability, mental status, and disposition to interaction. These particular findings were generally consistent with the findings from previous research.

Finally, we found that the participation of family members and friends was more closely associated—than the participation of the state relocation team—with the likelihood that an elderly person would survive the deleterious effects of relocation. Policy implications are discussed in Chapter 10.

APPENDIX

A Note on the Death Rates

In contrast to the years 1974 and 1975, the buildings housing Groups I and II did not have full occupancy during the year 1976. The building housing Group I was completely evacuated by August 31, 1976, and the building housing Group II was evacuated by the end of November, 1976. Based on eight months occupancy, with an average of thirty-six residents per month for Group I, four members, or eleven percent of the residents died in 1976. Or, stated another way, there were .5 deaths per month in Group I during the first eight months of the year 1976. At this rate, a total of six residents, or seventeen percent, would have died in Group I if the building had continued to house at least thirty-six residents per month for the full year. Since the years 1974 and 1975 were based on twelve months of occupancy, we thought it important to use a twelve month base for 1976, in order to minimize the risk of underestimating the death rate for 1976, when making comparisons with the other years and post-relocation data. As such, seventeen percent, rather than eleven percent, was used as the death rate for 1976, when comparisons were made between previous years and 1976, and between pre-relocation and post-relocation data.

Following the same line of reasoning for Group II, whose actual months of pre-relocation occupancy were the first eleven of 1976, we will use twenty-three percent instead of twenty-one percent as the comparative death rate for 1976. Our assumption is that building occupancy would have continued with an average of at least fifty-seven residents per month, had the building housing Group II continued in use for the entire year of 1976.

TABLE 6.3
Death Rates in Group I and Group II Between 1974 and 1976

GROUP I:	Monthly Residency	Deaths	%
1974	Average = 52	n = 11	21
1975	Average = 49	n = 9	18
1976	Average = 36	n = 4	17*
GROUP II:			
1974	Average = 70	n = 16	23
1975	Average = 70	n = 20	29
1976	Average = 57	n = 12	23**

* The last four months of the year 1976 are pro-rated for this group based on the average number of deaths per month for the first eight months of the year during which members of Group I were still occupying one of the buildings at Griot House.

** The last month, December 1976, was pro-rated for this group based on the average number of deaths per month for the first eleven months of the year during which members of Group II were still occupying the other building at Griot House.

Notes

1. At the inception of this study, there were eighty elderly members of Group II. Six, however, died before their physical relocation from Griot. Hence, there were 74 elderly persons in Group II when we began our post-relocation studies.
2. A methodological note. Ideally, the control for Group I in this study should have been a population of elderly blacks housed in a long-term care facility that had no chance of being selected as a target for relocation during the same period when Group I was moved. Group II was convenient for use in this study. But because of uncontrollable changes in the administrator's schedules for evacuation, the times for the relocation of Groups I and II eventually became so close that some degree of overlap was unavoidable. As a consequence, our comparison of death rates for Groups I and II did not permit as clear an analysis as we had hoped would be possible. Secondly, although several attempts had been made, by July of 1977, to secure accurate data from an alternate, predominantly black home (that could be used as a control for Group II), we were unsuccessful in that attempt.

CHAPTER 7

Black Elderly Residents
of Predominantly White Homes

A number of recent studies (Marlowe 1972; Yawney Slover 1973; Sherwood, Morris, and Barnhart 1975) have raised questions about the importance of the character and receptivity of established elderly residents of long-term care institutions into which new elderly inhabitants are moved. These studies suggest that the elderly person's feelings of comfort, in his or her new setting, may be an important determinant of his/her post-relocation adjustment. Although there has been little work on the effects of matching pre- and post-relocation environments and comfort index ratings of elderly persons in new settings, comments made by some of the elderly persons included in our study raised issues about the importance of ethnically homogeneous versus ethnically mixed receptor environments for previously institutionalized elderly persons. Some elderly specifically stated a preference to be moved to another setting that was generally populated, like their previous home, by other black elderly persons. Others showed no clear preference for a black home. Instead, their preferences were stated with particular attention to the race and/or general ethnic characteristics of prospective roommates, rather than the home in general. The latter preferences were especially pronounced where dormitory rooms seemed highly likely.

The potential significance of research on matching effects, and the practical difficulty of achieving pre- and post-relocation matching is suggested by some of the reactons of members of the Pennsylvania State Relocation Team, who were asked to respond to this particular request:

The patients have asked to be moved to nursing homes in the West Philadelphia, Germantown, and Mount Airy areas. The staff at Griot House wants nursing homes solicited which will welcome black patients and will understand black culture. There are relatively few homes which meet these criteria (O'Hara 1976, p. 2).

It seems clear in this excerpt, and in the studies cited above, that elderly attitudes toward the social characteristics of post-relocation environments are potentially important determinants of their post-relocation adjustment. In this chapter we will describe and analyze our findings on matching pre- and post-relocation residential settings.

Haphazard Versus Systematic Relocation Processes

In the design of this study, there was no control over the choice of the new settings for post-relocation residence of the elderly included. Nor were there any explicit indications that the Pennsylvania State Relocation Team was guided, in its selection of settings, by a primary concern with matching pre- and post-relocation settings by ethnic, race, and other hypothetical sociocultural correlates of personal adjustment. There was, of course, the acknowledgement of the potential significance of these factors as shown in the quotation on the preceding page. However, the identification of available beds, and the efficient relocation of the former inmates of Griot House seemed to take precedence over all other matters.

The Departments of Social Service and Nursing at Griot House showed much more vocal concern and concerted effort than the state relocation team in attempts to achieve pre- and post-relocation ethnic matching of residential settings. And, to a considerable extent, their efforts were successful. Forty-two of the former residents of old Griot House included in the study were moved into the new infirmary on the grounds of Griot House. In physical distance and degree of psychosocial disturbance experienced by them, through change from a known to an unknown social structure in the organization of everyday life, these elderly, no doubt, experienced the least stress. Furthermore, approximately ten persons were moved to private homes, either with relatives or black friends who were willing to accommodate an elderly boarder. Several others were moved to all black or predominantly black boarding homes to which other former residents of Griot House had gone before them, and whose administrators or managers had previously established close and supportive working relations with the staff and administrators of Griot House.

In this sketch, we have shown that the processes of relocating the elderly persons who we focused on were far less systematic, and guided by less planning focused on environmental matching, than that which might have been possible and desirable. However, it was not entirely haphazard.

Both the state relocation team and the staff of Griot House had their agendas. And, although they were not fully coordinated at every step in the relocation and followup on each resident, there was a modicum of success achieved by each. Furthermore, as we will show, the absence of ethnic matching did not necessarily mean negative outcomes for the physiological and psychosocial adjustments of all of the black elderly in our study.

Let us now take a closer look at our findings on the effects of matched and unmatched social environments. We will return in Chapter 10 for a closer look at the ideas of state relocation teams and other kinds of intervention systems in the residential relocation of elderly persons.

Withstanding Violations of Preferred
Social Distance from White Residential Settings

At the inception of this study, before any of these black elderly had experienced residential relocation, we found a significant difference in social distance scores between Groups I and II (t=2.24, p<.03). In the initial discussion that follows, we will focus on the adjustments made by members of these two groups, referred to as low distance and high distance groups, under conditons of relocation to predominantly black and predominantly white post-relocation residential settings.

Low distance will mean a group whose members, on the average, showed little or no preference for social distance from white persons in their new place of residence. By contrast, *high distance* will mean a group whose members showed marked preference for social distance from whites, ranging from a distaste for living in the same neighborhood to consenting to marry a white person.[1] To simplify the use of terms, black will be used to refer to predominantly black homes (fifty-one percent or more black residents) and white will be used to refer to predominantly white homes.

Self-image, Felt Agitation and Life Satisfaction

As might be expected, relocation to a black residential setting had no significant effect on the self-image of either the high or low distance groups. It was surprising, however, to find that relocation to white residential settings had significantly more negative influences on the self-imagery of the low distance group than it did on the high distance group (G=.42, n=42, p<.01). The low distance elderly also showed significantly higher levels of felt agitation than the high distance group under conditions of a white residential setting (G=.53, n=42, p<.01). By contrast, neither group showed significant change under conditions of relocation to a black setting. These results were surprising, in light of our initial findings of significant differences between the social distance scores of these two groups. We would have expected quite the opposite. It seems reasonable to expect that persons who have expressed a strong dislike for living with racially different others would display agitation and diminished self-imagery under conditions of forced relocation. However, our findings suggest that the high distance elderly may have entered what might be called a psychological cocoon, signified by an apparent withdrawal of cognitive attention and emotional sensitivity to the details of environmental changes occuring around them.

When we look at the low distance elderly, their reaction to the white settings were explained partly by their post-relocation attitudes toward those settings. While neither the high nor the low distance groups showed dislike for their new black homes, the low distance elderly who were moved to white settings showed significantly higher dislike for those settings than high distance blacks who were moved to similar places (G=.26, n=42, p<.01). This may be explained, in part, by the high degrees of anomia, or felt powerlessness and alienation, of the low distance elderly following their relocation to white residential settings.

It is not at all clear why the low distance elderly should register higher degrees of anomia than the high distance elderly, following relocation. If, however, the pre-relocation low distance scores represented a greater openness to whites and readiness for living side-by-side with them than that represented by high distance elderly, then the low distance elderly may have entered their new homes guided by many more illusions about their prospective caretakers and white co-residents than their high distance counterparts. For example, many interview protocols of low distance elderly contained remarks expressing the sentiments that the black elderly person "would not mind living with a white roommate" as long as "I'm treated right."[2] However, the adjustments made by most were not characterized by easy entry into new friendships and mutual support relations with new peers. For example, we found that low distance elderly had no more success than high distance elderly in forming new friendships in white homes.

The apparently closed social relations among whites, and the negative attitude of blacks toward those settings was distinguished by a decidedly more positive reaction of low distance elderly to new black homes. For example, whereas relocation to a white home had no significant influence on the sense of life satisfaction for low ditance groups, it had a somewhat negative influence on the high distance group (G=.45, n=30, p<.01). For the high distance elderly, who for the most part strongly resisted change, their declining life satisfaction scores may have signified their general displeasure with residential change. Whereas the more integrationist, low distance elderly, who also showed less opposition to residential change, may have signified (by their high satisfaction scores) their pleasure that the changes for them—from one black setting to another—had been far less radical than expected.

Overall, whether high or low in social distance scores, the black elderly in this study showed a tendency toward higher levels of morale when moved to another black, rather than a white, residential setting. Table 7.1 is illustrative. Generally, the results described in the foregoing discussion are mixed. However, the black elderly who expressed a pre-relocation preference for high social distance from whites seemed to have made a better adjustment than low distance elderly, whether placed in a black or a white residential setting.

TABLE 7.1

Relationship Between Race of Post-Relocation Environment and Morale of Black Elderly Persons Moving From an All-Black to a White Residential Setting

| | Race of a New Home | |
Morale	Black	White
High	57%	47%
Low	43%	53%
N (66)	28	38

Social Distance and Visiting Behavior

Consistent with the implicit preference for living among blacks, the high distance group was significantly more outgoing than the low distance group under conditions of settlement in another black home (G=.40, n=54, p<.01). Neither group, however, was significantly outgoing under conditions of life in a white residential setting.

The differences between these groups in ratings of mental status may help to explain the variations in their interaction patterns. Under both the white and black residential conditions, there were significant differences between the high and low distance groups in post-relocation levels of mental status (X^2=7.71, df=3, p <.05; X^2=11.84, df=4, p <.02, respectively). Since the differences were sharpest in the black settings, we can be relatively comfortable in setting aside the prospect of white rater bias. In other words, if one or another set of nurses' ratings of mental status represented cultural biases, it was clearly in the direction of the black, and not the white homes.

Secondly, the high distance elderly received higher ratings on mental status than the low distance elderly in black and white homes, with the sharpest manifest differences between them in their post-relocation black homes (G=.38, n=54, p<.01). Since high mental status is characterized by clear articulation of speech, and little or no mental confusion and forgetfulness, it is reasonable to assume that high distance elderly characterized by high mental status would be more outgoing than their low distance, low mental status counterparts. However, there is no straightforward explanation for the significantly low levels of mental status of the low distance elderly. There were no significant differences between the high distance and low distance groups preceding relocation, nor were there differences between them, in general, immediately following relocation. On the surface, it appears that the differences between them were related to the differences between their abilities to adjust to their post-relocation homes. And, those high distance black elderly who survived the first four months of residential change seemed to make the best overall adjustment.

High Distance Elderly Blacks and Friendship Behavior

While there were no differences between the high and low distance elderly in making new friends in white homes, the high distance elderly were significantly more active (than their low distance counterparts) in forming new friendships in new black residential settings (G=.44, n=30, p< .01). Furthermore, the high distance elderly in black homes were significantly likely to see their friends more often than the low distance elderly would (G=.29, n=30, p <.01). Even more striking was the high association (G=.66), n=43, p<.001) between low distance elderly moving to white residential settings and the decreasing incidence in the frequency with which they saw old friends. There are a number of possible interpretations for this state of affairs.

First of all, three of the predominantly white settings, to which forty percent of the coherent elderly were moved, were located outside the city of Philadelphia (where our study groups lived before their relocation). No doubt, the increase in geographical distance from the city where old friends lived had a decisive impact on the decreasing frequency of visits from those friends. Considering the significance of friends and friendly visits in determining personal adjustment to the uncertainties of everyday life, the increased residential distance from old friends may help to explain the decline in mental status, self-image, and life satisfaction of low distance elderly in white homes.

There were also marked decreases in visits from family members to low distance blacks. Low distance elderly who moved to white homes experienced significant decreases in frequency of visits from family members (G=.34, n=43, p <.01). By contrast, low distance elderly who moved to another black home showed significant increases, not decreases, in frequencies of visits from family members (G=.30, n=30, p<.05). While there were related decrements in visits received by high distance elderly in white homes and increases in visits in black homes, in neither case were the changes for them as sharp as they were for low distance blacks.

Secondly, the individually perceived decline in frequency of visits received by members of the low distance group in white residential settings (G=.36, n=43, p <.01) was closely associated with their increased sense of distance from old friends. The increased geographical distance of most of the new white homes from old Philadelphia neighborhoods was indisputable. Much less clear was the extent to which the new residential setting of the low distance groups might have been unacceptable to their friends. For example, high social distance friends (of the low distance elderly relocated in this study) could have objected to the choice of a white home for, or by, their former friends. Furthermore, they might have expressed their distaste by a diminishing frequency of visits. Unfortunately, we did not have measures of attitudes of friends toward the post-relocation homes of the elderly involved in the relocation process. As such, we could not empirically assess the merits of this hypothesis. Nevertheless, it fits intuitively with other studies of patterns of social exclusion (Foucault 1965; Dubois 1926).

Summary

In an involuntary movement of members of one ethnic group into a setting predominantly populated by members of another, made in spite of a high distaste of the former for close relations with the latter (as measured by the Bogardus social distance scale), we should expect significantly more signs of distress than we would under conditions where persons were permitted to move to a new setting housing members of their own ethnic group. In our study, we found some support for this conclusion. Black elderly who moved to black homes showed generally higher levels of morale than black elderly who moved to white homes. However, the results were not as simple to interpret as this conclusion may suggest.

The black elderly who showed high pre-relocation preferences for social distance from whites also showed significantly better personal adjustment to black homes than those elderly who showed a low preference for social distance from whites. Furthermore, the high distance elderly also faired relatively well in white homes. Their levels of self-image, felt agitation, and life satisfaction were not significantly different from those reported for low distance elderly under the same conditions. A number of alternative explanations were offered to account for these unexpected findings. Sustained relations with friends, made possible by new homes that were geographically closer to older neighborhoods and friends, and lower expectations of open, congenial relations with whites (in contrast to the low distance blacks) may have helped to explain the relatively positive adjustments of the high distance elderly. We turn now to examine other aspects of the social structure and the social psychology of coping with stress, focusing in particular on religiosity, and other variables that intervene between the individual and environmental change to help explain his/her patterns of adjustment.

Note

1. For the original version of "The Social Distance Scale," used in this study, see Emory S. Bogardus, "A Social Distance Scale," *Sociology and Social Research* 17, 3 (January-February 1933): pp. 265-271.

CHAPTER 8

Perceived Locus of Control of Environmental Change and Personal Adjustment

In most of the previous research that has focused on relocation stress among elderly persons, a number of potentially important factors have either been omitted or given only scant attention. Little attention has been given to preadmission differences in social class background (Storandt, Wittels, and Botwinick 1975) and the degrees of importance assigned by the elderly to their relative control over change in the order of things—especially felt powerlessness to regulate social and physical environmental changes that have direct effects on their life situations (Marlowe 1972). Furthermore, while there may be variations in lifestyle that help to differentiate survivors from nonsurvivors of forced social migration (Watson and Maxwell 1977; Riley, Johnson, and Foner 1971; Miller and Lieberman 1965), little of the research to date has focused on the significance of this factor.

Low income inner-city elderly, such as most of those persons in our study, may have been faced throughout much of their lives with unemployment or underemployment, and frequent changes in place of residence. And among those whose life-sustaining resources—such as food, shelter and clothing—were secured through daily struggles in a harsh pre-admission social environment, there may have been considerably higher survival rates than those rates found among members of other groups on first admission to a home, hospital, or another specialized setting for the elderly.

On the other hand, there may be class-related differences between world views (Yawney and Slover 1973; Fried 1963), in which lower class elderly, with a relatively limited and neighborhood based outlook, may manifest more grief than higher class elderly, whose broader world views permit a perceptual transcendence of particularistic environments, making social change less traumatic for them. In this chapter we will study in detail the influences of physical self-maintenance ability, length of residence in a new home, social class background, and religiosity on the social and psychological adjustments of elderly blacks in a new residential setting.

Social Change

In the context of change in place of residence, there may be corresponding changes in the demographic composition of the group in which the migrant then becomes a member. New social relations must be formed. For example, an elderly black migrant may become a member of a predominantly white, or a previously all white group, in a long-term care facility exposed to one or more black persons for the first time. In so far as race-related stereotypes and beliefs are operative, each will have to make certain adjustments to the other. The effects of these kinds of changes in personality and social behavior may be many and varied in degree. Selected social and psychological effects of changes in residence from a predominantly black to a predominantly white setting will be examined closely in the analysis that follows. Social change will be represented by alternations in the characteristics of members or the population of a group sharing a common residential setting.

Social change can also be represented by shifts in relations between persons. Persons who have enjoyed frequent interactions with family and friends may experience a decline in the frequency of visits and opportunities for those interactions as a consequence of increased distance from the previous place of residence and/or location of interaction. Residential relocation to a new city, a suburban area, or a new neighborhood within the same city, can strain a previous relation with another person or group who does not relocate at the same time and to the same place. The subsequent decline in social interaction can have deleterious effects on the post-migrational, social and psychological functioning of the person. Some of these kinds of changes will be described and discussed in this chapter and the next.

Physiological and Social Structures
of Adjustment to Social Change

We will focus, in general, on some evidence of the influences of social change on the social and psychological behavior of elderly black persons.

We will also study various factors that help to regulate or structure the behavior of the black elderly under conditions of social change. First, we will study some findings of the relationship between adjustments to forced migration and pre-relocation levels of physical self-maintenance ability. Then we will study the relationship between various aspects of personal adjustment and length of residence in a new home, social class background, and religiosity.

Physical Self-maintenance Ability

In previous research (Lawton and Yaffe 1970), it was suggested that high pre-relocation levels of physical self-maintenance ability would be conducive to positive post-relocation adjustments. In comparing our pre- and post-relocation measures of morale, as determined by the PGC Morale Scale, we found significant support for this hypothesis in persons ranked high in physical self-maintenance in Phase I (t=2.33, p< .027). By contrast, Phase I persons who ranked low in physical self-maintenance showed no significant change in morale scores over time.

Persons previously ranked high in physical self-maitenance ability also showed significant increases in their level of life satisfaction (t=3.80, p< .001). By contrast, there was no significant change in the level of life satisfaction among persons ranked low in physical self-maintenance.

Neither high nor low physical self-maintenance groups showed change in attitudes toward their own aging. There were, however, some puzzling changes in the low physical self-maintenance group following its relocation. For example, there were significant decreases in the sense of anomia (t=2.32, p < .025), and felt agitation (t=2.76, p <.009). By contrast, there were no significant changes in these measures for the high physical self-maintenance group. We will examine these findings in more detail below.

Length of Residence and Psychosocial Adjustment

Generally, we found that social change had its greatest negative influence on personal functioning immediately following relocation. There were sharp increases in signs of agitation (G=.33, n=71, p<.01),and increased levels of loneliness and life dissatisfaction (G=.23, n=71, p<.01). Greater lengths of residence in a new setting were directly related to greater improvements in all measures of personal functioning. Levels of overall morale improved with lengths of residence (G=.51, n=71, p<.001) However, length of residence was not significantly related to anomia.

It should be noted that the correlations between length of residence and improvements in levels of personal adjustment do not necessarily mean that these black elderly persons were personally shifting back toward pre-relocation levels of psychological functioning. In fact, all of the tests with a focus on the personal functioning of these elderly people, as measured by change in felt agitation, self-image, loneliness, and other factors, showed that their levels of functioning were consistently higher, on all measures, after relocation. However, for the full sample of seventy persons we had measured, the only statistically significant changes were found in decreased levels of agitation and increased levels of morale following relocation.

There were several possible interpretations for these findings. Although the anticipation of relocation or of being uprooted was apparently traumatic—as suggested by the significantly high degree of pre-relocation agitation (t=2.79, p<.007), and the increased death rate shown in Figure 1 of Chapter 6—the actual experiences of the relocation process and the new residential settings were apparently much less traumatic than anticipated. In fact, a test of the relationship betweeen length of residence in the new settings and perceptions of positive changes in life situation showed a weak, but statistically significant association (G=.30, n=72, p<.01). Generally, these findings showed that change for these black elderly was far more positive than traumatic in social and psychological rewards.

The Significance of Social Class

As we showed in Chapter 2, there were pre-admission differences in economic and educational classes among the elderly in this study. In Chapter 2 economic status and educational status were treated as separate variables. We have combined those factors in this chapter to form a composite measure of socioeconomic status. Based on the composite measure that we formed, the seventy persons whom we interviewed were distributed into the following subclasses: (1) seventeen percent were included in the upper-lower class, (2) thirty-nine percent were included in the middle-lower class, and (3) forty-four percent were included in the lower-lower class.

Among the black elderly at upper-lower and lower-lower class levels, there were no significant changes in self-image, agitation, loneliness-dissatisfaction, and general morale during the relocation process. However, lower-middle class elderly showed significant decreases in level of felt agitation (T=2.64, p<.014) and improvements in general morale (t=2.16, p<.05). This finding is inconsistant with the Yawney and Slover (1973) and Fried (1963) hypotheses suggesting a unilinear relationship between class level and adjustment to social change. A curvilinear interpretation is more consistent with our findings. However, it is not at all clear how or why this relationship should exist.

In our post-relocation analyses of variations in self-image, felt agitation, and loneliness and life dissatisfaction, our composite measures of SES failed to explain any of the post-relocation variations in these scores.

However when we re-examined these data, using a subjective measure of economic status (self-perceived economic status), the results were sharply different. A high self-perceived economic status was significantly related to high self-image (G=.37, n=72, p<.001) and sense of life satisfaction (G=.62, n=72, p<.001). There was also a weak relationship between high self-perceived economic status and decreasing feelings of agitation (G=.17, n=72, p<.05). High self-perceived economic status was also significantly related to high post-relocation levels of morale (G=.37, n=72, p<.01).

The absence of a relationship between our composite measure of SES and the various aspects of personal adjustment may be partly due to the fact that we included level of education in the composite measure. We have already shown, in Chapter 3, the negligible explanatory value of education—as opposed to economic status—in our attempt to understand the self-imagery of black elderly people. We reasoned in Chapters 2 and 3 that the history of dejure and defacto racial segregation in public accommodations (including education), in combination with other pervasive structures of the social oppression of blacks between 1880 and 1954, probably ruled out or minimized any appreciable effect that post-elementary school education could have had on the socioeconomic mobility, self-imagery, and general sense of social and psychological well-being of black Americans. All of the elderly in our study were born and raised during that period and, in all likelihood, were not spared from its racially discriminatory effects.

Secondly, elderly people, mental patients, and others in long-term care institutions are seldom responsible (except in token ways) for their own financial affairs in the everyday life of their residential settings. Most, if not all of their costs, are paid by state custodians, guardians, family members, or other individuals or institutions. As such, it is reasonable to expect (in the judgements made by elderly persons) a decreasing awareness of the economic facts, and a decreasing accuracy in perception of the "real" costs of long-term care. In so far as measures of socioeconomic status are concerned in studies of elderly in long-term care institutions, as the length of residence increases and the responsibility for socioeconomic decision-making decreases, the criteria of objective measures of socioeconomic status may become more remote from the everyday lives of the elderly, and consequently less valid as independent variables used in attempts to explain the psychological behavior of the inmates. Subjective measures, such as self-perceived economic status, and reputational techniques, defined by rankings that elderly or inmate peers make of each other, may be more useful.[1]

Finally, the measure of socioeconomic class that we used, like other "objective" measures of SES in the social sciences, was based on relatively static factors. We used social history and intake data from the Department of Social Services at Griot House, and data made available by the medical records librarian. The indices included were the highest levels of formal education recorded, plus the way in which the costs of long-term care were paid. Many changes had occurred in the lives of these elderly blacks since moving to Griot House, not the least of which was their relocation to a new place of residence. Unlike the composite measure of SES that focused on the static factors, the measure of self-perceived economic change reflected the elderly person's sense of improvement (or lack thereof) in economic status, in association with his or her residential change. To the extent that there were real and/or imagined improvements in socioeconomic class associated with residential change, it was reasonable to expect that a

TABLE 8.1

Relationship Between Pre-Relocation Importance Assigned to Religion and Personal Adjustment to Stressors Associated with Change in Place of Residence of a Group of Elderly Black People+

Importance Assigned to Religion**	Aspects of Personal Adjustment	Pre-Reloc. Average Scores	4 Month Post Reloc Average Scores	t-Value	2 Tail Prob.
Very Important (N=31)	Self Image	1.290	1.548	- .74	.463
	Felt Agitation	3.677	5.097	-2.86	.008*
	Loneliness	2.581	3.323	-2.56	.016*
	Morale	3.516	4.742	-2.75	.010*
	Anomia	2.290	2.258	.10	.921
Somewhat Important (N=10)	Self Image	2.100	1.300	1.35	.210
	Felt Agitation	5.200	4.400	1.21	.259
	Loneliness	3.100	2.700	.77	.462
	Morale	4.900	4.000	2.08	.068*
	Anomia	2.000	2.900	-1.65	.134

*The probability that mean differences this large or larger could occur by chance variation is equal to or less than 10/100.

**There were only two persons who assigned no importance to religion. A sample this small was too little to permit meaningful statistical analysis.

+For anomia, high scores indicate negative personal adjustment. For all other indicators, high average scores represent positive personal adjustment.

measure of SES that detected change would be a far more discriminating and valid measure. An instrument based on static external indices, in studies of social change important to the elderly in the organization of their everyday lives, would certainly be less discriminating and less valid.

It should also be noted that the reported perception of change in economic status may indirectly reflect the improved living conditions, rather than increased personal income, or other individulaized elements of economic status. Many of the new homes were much more modern than Griot House. Most of the new residential settings had better interior lighting, brighter and more colorful decor, and other amenities. Some elderly persons even reported better meals, and were able to get out of doors and dress up more often. These were changes that would ordinarily require improvement in individual economic resources, a redistribution of existing resources, or new revenues of owners of homes.

Where residents handle very little money and do very little economic bargaining in their own self-interest (which is probably the case for most chronically ill residents of long-term care institutions), the sense of improvement in economic well-being will probably vary directly with the visibility of new investments and material improvements in the social and architectural environment—made by the owner of the facility. Following this line of reasoning, the self-perceived changes in economic status probably reflected improvements in the new housing for the elderly and selected supportive services, rather than improvements in individual economic resources. This conclusion seems especially reasonable under circumstances where the "real" economic resources of the elderly inmate are held constant.

In summary, self-perceived changes in economic status reported by residents of long-term care institutions may be understood to be functions of increases in extra-individual supplies of highly desired goods—such as better food, shelter and clothing—relative to the previously real or imagined resources that were owned or made accessible to the individual resident, and by which he or she could purchase or command a share of the desired goods and services.

Religiosity, Perceived Locus of Control of Individual Action and Adjustment to Social Change

For our final consideration in this chapter, we will describe and analyze some findings about the relations between religiosity and personal adjustment under conditions of change in place of residence. By religiosity, we mean the importance assigned by the elderly to religious activity, such as prayer and bible reading, and their frequency of church attendance.

Since we are primarily concerned with isolating pre-relocation predictors of adjustment to social change, we focused on pre-relocation measures of religiosity. We expected to find a positive relationship between high pre-change religiosity and high post-change adjustment.

Persons who assigned the highest pre-relocation importance to religion were the only ones who showed significantly positive levels of adjustment following change in place of residence. Table 8.1 demonstrates that persons high in pre-relocation religiosity registered significantly lower levels of post-relocation feelings of agitation, and higher levels of life satisfaction and morale, when comparisons were made between their pre-relocation and post-relocation measures. Although the differences were not statistically significant, the average scores for post-relocation measures of attitudes toward own aging were also much higher, in the high religiosity group, than they were in the other two subgroups representing lower degrees of religiosity.

We also found that the declining level of post-relocation morale among low religiosity elderly was inversely related to increased levels of anomia among them. While the changes in anomia scores were not statistically significant, the pattern was clear. Figure 8.1 is illustrative.

It should be noted, as shown in Figure 8.1, that the improvements in morale in the high religiosity group were not associated with corresponding decreases in anomia. In fact, there was no change in anomia in the high religiosity group. However, the decreasing level of morale in the low religiosity group was associated with an increasingly higher level of anomia.

Perceived Locus of Control of Individual and Social Action

The increasing degree of anomia among low religiosity elderly blacks, in association with residential relocation, may signify their felt powerlessness to control or regulate their lives and the changing social environments. Following the research findings on locus of control of change in aspects of the social environmnt and its influence upon the person, this interpretation is reasonable. According to the theory and research on the perceived internal versus external locus of control of action (Rotter 1943, pp. 254-274; 1966; Gore and Rotter 1963; Sampson 1971, pp. 324-326):

> Persons called externals characteristically view themselves as lacking control over their environment. Things happen to them; rewards are just given to them, as are punishments; and there is little they feel they can do about controlling these reinforcements. Internals generally see themselves as in control of things in their environments; specifically, they feel themselves capable of creating conditions that yield positive reinforcements or avoid negative reinforcements. (Sampson 1971, p. 324).

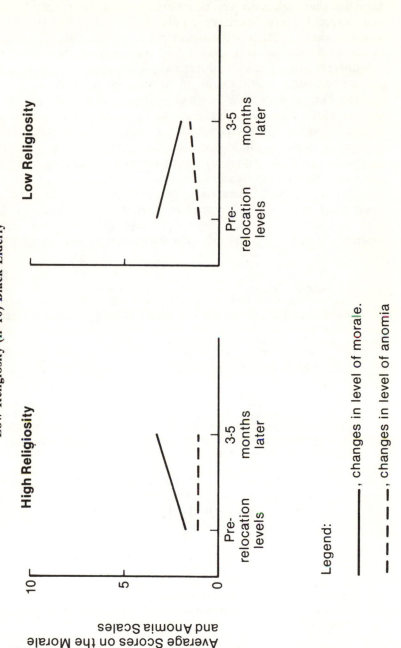

FIGURE 8.1

Social Change, Stress, and Change in Levels of Morale and Anomia in a Group of High Religiosity (n=31) and Low Religiosity (n=10) Black Elderly

Legend:

———————, changes in level of morale.

— — — — —, changes in level of anomia

Assuming that high religiosity elders are also high in external locus, we would expect them to experience less distress than highly internal and low religiosity elders under conditions of involuntary relocation. The externals expect little control and should find unexpected changes in their environment less stressful than internals, who expect control over their environment and participation in decision-making about planned changes. Further, assuming that high religiosity is an indicator of high externality, it is reasonable to expect—as we found—very little change in anomia for high religiosity elderly under conditions of involuntary change in place of residence. It follows that the opposite would hold, as we demonstrated, for low religiosity elderly persons who are highly internal, rather than external, in locus of contrtol.

As shown in Table 8.1, the majority of the elderly (supplying us with self-report data) in this study were high in religiosity. The following excerpt from an interview with an eighty-eight year old gentleman helps to illustrate the extent of religiously oriented externality among these black elderly persons:

> Man is only a subject; a, ah, part of a mission that God created for Himself. Man was made for Him (God). He didn't make nothing. How could he create? Man didn't create anything. Man only used what God put here for him.

From the point of view of an eighty-seven year old black woman, we gain further insight into the relationship between religiosity and external locus of control:

> When I come from North Carolina to Philadelphia, I joined Whalen Temple. And I stayed there a while. And, I wanted to go yonder to the Met. That is where the Spirit led me. And I went there; and my spirit examined that church before I joined there.

The examination of the church, and apparent approval by her spirit, was a personal pre-condition for her joining. The significance of her spiritual beliefs are even more striking in her comments about the burial of her body after death, and quality of her soul in the "eyes" of her God:

> Ain't no use to carry the body back down south. Don't worry about the body. Get the soul right. God will take care of that. The earth will sure take care of the body. Ha! Ha! Ha! My spirit showed me my robe and my crown. It was the finest thing I ever saw. My crown was planted with bright stars. My intention and determination is to hold out to the end. Just like a person lives; just like they die.

These kinds of themes and some minor variations were recurrent throughout the interviews with these elderly black persons. As suggested by one of the more highly educated black elderly males in our study (a doctor of podiatric medicine), religiosity may be far more important and pervasive, in its influences on the behavior of black elders, than we have yet begun to realize:

> The Negro Church is important because I think the ideals generated (by it) are needed. And I think there are many people who wouldn't be very amenable to law and order, or even have the larger view of life; of love and understanding, if it (the Negro church) were not there; if they weren't touched.

As this old gentleman suggested further on in the interview, and in the last five lines of this excerpt, the church, and the beliefs of blacks in the teachings of the church, have played an important part in buttressing respect for law and order in American society. And, in the absence of the black church, and the deeply spiritual underpinnings growing out of it that helped to form the structure of social order among blacks, there probably would have been far less tolerance of the conditions of racism and economic exploitation during their lifetimes, just as there was a lower degree of tolerance of relocation stress among low religiosity people in this study.

Finally, when we examined separately the relationship between pre-relocation frequencies of church attendance and post-relocation indicators of personal adjustment, we found no significant decrements or improvements in post-relocation personal adjustment, except for persons who reported that they never went to church before residential relocation. On the surface, this was puzzling. Earlier, as reported in Chapter 4, we had found a positive relationship between the value assigned to religion and frequency of church attendance in both samples selected for this study (G=.71 and .85, respectively). And, just as persons who were high in their pre-relocation valuation of religion showed significant improvements in personal adjustment following residential change, we expected a similar finding in the relationship between pre-relocation church attendance and subsequent personal adjustment.

However, persons who never went to church may have warranted separate analysis. For example, the absence of church attendance was not necessarily associated with the assignment of a low value to religion. Instead, as we showed in Chapter 4, low physical self-maintenance ability was closely associated with low frequencies of church attendance (G=.40, n=.52, p < .01). As such, while physical disability may frustrate church attendance, it will not necessarily diminish religiosity.

Secondly, persons who never went to church, perhaps because of severe physical disability, may have shown significant improvements in self-

TABLE 8.2
Indicators of Improvements in the Personal Adjustment
of Church Non-Attenders in New Residential Settings[+]

Aspects of Personal Adjustment	Pre-relocation (Average Scores)	Four Months After Relocation (Average Scores)	t-values	2 Tail Prob.
Self Image	1.143	2.500	-2.46	.028*
Felt Agitation	4.357	5.714	-1.69	.115
Loneliness/dis.	2.071	3.571	-3.50	.004*
Morale	3.357	5.643	-3.35	.005*
Anomia	2.133	2.533	-1.15	.271
Disposition to Interaction	8.733	9.800	-2.48	.027
Mental Status	8.867	10.333	-2.90	.012*
Self Maint. Ability	47.133	50.867	-2.80	.014*

* Average differences that are much greater than that would be expected by chance.

+ For anomia, high scores indicate negative personal adjustment. For all other indicators, high average scores represent positive personal adjustment.

image, general morale, and other aspects of personal adjustment for nonreligious reasons. Table 8.2 illustrates the characteristics of personal adjustment in which there were significant changes. Considering the fact that persons who never went to church were also low in pre-relocation religiosity, their improvements in personal adjustment, following residential change, may have been far more closely associated with the material improvements—in the food, shelter, and other nonreligious services—received by them in their new homes, than with the significance of religious beliefs (that was so clearly paramount for the elderly persons on the opposite end of the religiosity continuum). As we suggested earlier in our discussion of the influences of socioeconomic factors, the real improvements in housing and services that occurred for many of these elderly through residential relocation, probably had an immeasurably positive impact on their post-relocation adjustment.

Summary

In this chapter, we studied the realtionship between change in place of residence and other aspects of the social environment, and personal adjustments of elderly black persons. We isolated two important pre-relocation variables intervening between the factors of residential change and personal adjustment. The most significant intervening variables helping to explain positive post-relocation adjustment were high pre-relocation physical self-maintenance ability, and high religiosity (or value assigned to the importance of religion). Associated with these pre-relocation predictors of adjustment were another set of significant intervening variables: These were (1) the elderly person's self-perceived improvement in his/her post-relocation means of economic subsistence, and (2) length of residence in the new home. Consistent with our hunch, formulated in Chapter 3, we found increasing improvements in personal adjustment in association with increased length of residence. We found no relationship between pre-relocation objective measures of socioeconomic class and post-relocation adjustment. We turn now to a study of the importance of family and friends in the social structure and coping behavior of black elderly persons undergoing relocation stress. *199870*

Note

1. Please write the author for details about the "self-perceived change questionnaire."

CHAPTER 9

Families and Friends in
the Reduction of Relocation Stress

There is an abundance of research demonstrating the importance of family members and kinship networks as buffers—against environmental stressors that impinge upon and endanger the lives and psychological well-being of family members (Billingsley 1968; Hill 1972; Durkheim 1951; Watson 1969). Through the socially solidary relations between persons that are possible in family and friendship groups, individual experiences of potentially traumatic events are frequently less personally disconcerting.

As we showed in Chapters 5, 7, and 8, elderly persons who had close relations with offspring, other family members, and friends reported significantly higher levels of self-image and sense of life satisfaction, and lower levels of felt agitation, than persons who seldom received visits from any of these kinds of significant others. As a result of the clear and significant relationships found between those and other factors related to the behavior of the black elderly before their relocation, we decided to examine more closely the intensity of primary group interaction in post-relocation patterns of personal adjustment.

Intensity of Primary Group
Interaction and Personal Adjustment

Intensity of interaction was defined by the frequency of visits made between an elderly person and members of various categories of other persons (including friends, offspring, and other relatives). Based on a simple frequency distribution, intensity could range from zero (or no visits) to an indefinite upper limit.

We used three different questionnaire items to construct our intensity measure. In our "self-perceived change questionnaire," the relocated elderly participants were asked to rate, from better to worse, the extent to which there had been changes in the frequency with which offspring, other relatives and friends made visits to see them. The separate responses to each question were then added together to form an intensity score. As we predicted in the pre-relocation phase of this study (Chapter 5), we found that elderly blacks with intensive post-relocation primary group relations had significantly higher levels of self-imagery (G=.43, n=72, p<.01), and sense of life satisfaction (G=.40, n=73, p<.01) than elderly persons who reported weak primary group relations. Similarly, there was a significant positive relationship between intensity of post-relocation primary group relations and the overall morale of these elderly persons (G=.34, n=72, p<.01).

It was interesting to note that the general variable—of intensity of primary group interaction—explained very little of the variance in felt agitation following relocation (G=.17, n=72). By contrast, when we partialed out frequent visits from old friends (including other elders who moved to the same post-relocation place of residence, and former members of the staff who were known at Griot House), there were significantly lower degrees of post-relocation agitation (G= —.60, n=53, p < .001). This finding, and those reported above, gave further support to our earlier observation about the overall significance of friendly visitors in the social and psychological adjustment of elderly persons living in long-term care institutions.

Frequent visits—from offspring, other relatives, and aged friends, in their new places of residence—were also significantly related to positive attitudes of the elderly toward their new homes (G=.40, n=69, p < .01). Frequent visits by offspring and other relatives may have functioned as a symbolic ratification of the propriety of the new residential setting, and assured the elderly person that he or she had made, or been a part of, a wise choice of new housing. By contrast, visits from old friends—who did not move to the new place of residence—contributed much less to the explanation of the attitudes of the elderly toward their new homes (G=.26, n=52, p < .01).

These findings suggested that sustained ties with external or extra-institutional friends may be much less important than relations with inmate friends as determinants of the elderly person's attitude toward his new home. In a sense, elderly peers in long-term care, who become the objects of involuntary relocation, may look less often to outside significant others (than they look to each other) for reassurance that their changes in place of residence will have positive outcomes for them.

Primary group interactions can also function, under these circumstances, as structural buffers between elderly persons and the stresses associated with adjustment to a new home. Through visiting behavior and the interactions that unfold in visits, old and cherished values are reasserted and relations renewed between persons. These may take on greater importance at the time that psychological distress is being experienced through—what may seem to be—unpredictable changes in their social environment.

An indication—of the depth of the bonds with extra-institutional members of primary groups—is shown by the absence of a relationship between length of residence in new settings and intensity of primary group interaction. The monthly frequency of visits and perceived flux in primary group relations were relatively constant, over the several months following residential change, for the elderly in this study. By contrast, the intensity of interaction with old friends who also moved to the new place of residence showed significant increases with increasing length in the new settings ($G = - .80$, $n=52$, $p < .001$). The latter finding probably reflects the initial, post-relocation preoccupation of the elderly with becoming familiar with their new homes. In a sense, each elderly person had to make his/her own psychosocial adjustment to the "new home," as it were, gradually begin to explore relations with other persons, and re-establish old ties, where possible.

Aged Peers, Old Friends, and the Perception of New Residential Settings

Just as frequent visits from primary group members helped to sustain their positive self-imagery, sense of life satisfaction, and generally high levels of morale, such visits improved the perspectives of these black elderly persons on their new residential settings. Generally, there were higher levels of self-perceived health with increasing frequencies of visits from extra-institutional members of primary groups ($G=.33$, $n=73$, $p < .01$). Even more significant was the relationship between self-perceived health and visits from old Griot House friends who moved to the same place of residence ($G=.51$, $n=33$, $p < .001$).

We also found clear differences, between members of extra-institutional primary groups and old friends, on two other health-related factors in post-relocation behavior: These were patterns in eating and sleeping behavior. Visits from members of extra-institutional primary groups had no bearing on eating and sleeping behavior. However, there were significant increases in the reported quality of the food service, and participation in scheduled meals by individual elderly, in association with increases in the frequency of visits from old Griot House friends (G=.32, n=53, p < .01). Similarly, visits from extra-institutional members of primary groups had no bearing on post-relocation sleeping behavior, but visits from old Griot House friends did: the more frequent the visits from old friends (aged peers), the higher the quality of reported sleeping behavior (G.41, n=53, p <.01). We found no straightforward reason why visits from aged peers, in contrast to visits from members of extra-institutional primary groups, should have a marked influence on self-perceived health, eating, and sleeping behavior. However, the differences are worth speculating about.

Interpersonal Relations Between Elderly
Inmates of Long-term Care Institutions

The elderly person's feeling of being or not being healthy, and his/her eating and sleeping behavior, are much more intricately connected with the internal order of a home for the aged than the social organization of behavior on the outside. Offspring, other relatives, and extra-institutional friends are probably seldom around when medicines and prescribed treatments are dispensed, food is being served, and the elderly inmate is bedded down. By contrast, elderly residential peers, such as old friends from Griot House, who are likely to be included as bedtime roommates, mealtime table-mates, or discussants in lounge areas, are likely to be accessible on a daily basis and recognized by the elderly as persons equally familiar and on similarly intimate terms, with the internal situations of institutional living. As such, inmate-friends, especially those with whom a long-term relationship has been sustained through the crisis of relocation stress, are much more likely to be regarded as significant others. Their judgements on matters pertaining to the intricacies of everyday life are likely to have much greater influence on the thoughts and feelings of other inmates than the judgements of outsiders. It follows, then, that members of extra-institutional primary groups should have a considerably greater influence on inmate behaviors in extra-institutional places (such as shopping trips and outside visits), than they do on those events and places that are central to the inner world of long-term care institutions.

Visits by Extra-institutional Primary
Groups and the Behavior of Elderly Inmates

Self-reported increases in activity level, opportunities to get out (go places outside the residential setting) and to "dress up" are consistently and significantly related to visits from extra-institutional primary groups—not aged peers and friends living in a home (G=.39, n=73, p < .01). These findings are not surprising.

Seldom, if ever, in homes for the elderly or other places designed for the long-term care of the chronically ill, are inmates permitted to wander or leave the premises as they wish (Watson and Maxwell 1977; Goffman 1961; Foucault 1965). Much more commonly, their egress to places on the outside is a consequence of either special programs—planned by social service staff, group therapeutic, recreational or other specialists—or lapses in the surveillance of their movements by gatekeepers. Opportunities for getting outside may also occur as a consequence of visits from offspring, other relatives, or extra-institutional friends who arrange the opportunity, and accept the responsibility for the welfare of the elderly inmate while on the outside.

In so far as an expected visit from an extra-institutional primary group member is a pleasant occasion for the elderly inmate (perhaps because it signals an opportunity for a temporary escape from the inmate world), then significant increases in both activity level (G=.49, n=73, p <.01) and reported "happiness" (G=.58, n=73, p <.01) are to be expected in association with increased frequencies of those kind of visits. By contrast, visits from aged peers and old Griot House friends living in the same post-residential setting should have, as we found, no measurable influence on activity level and self-reported happiness.

There were other findings that further corroborated the differences between the influences of outside and inside significant others. We have already shown that high frequencies of visits from members of extra-institutional primary groups were significantly related to "dressing up" behavior (G=.39, n=73, p < .01). By contrast, there was no relationship between dressing up and visits from inmate friends. Dressing up signifies a kind of behavior that occurs in association with a person's preparation for entry into a public place. And, as one of our elderly interviewees observed, "on very special occasions, such as holy days, dressing up may be quite elaborately done."

> Even canes were used, especially on Sunday afternoon. They might be wearing overalls or old clothes on their jobs (weekdays). But on Sunday, man, they had to dress up; and, man, they had capes. They were dressed in their latest fashion. They were more conservative and yet, they were well dressed in quality materials.

The importance assigned to dressing up and getting out on Sundays and holidays is not peculiar to modern times or the elderly blacks observed in this study. As suggested in a recent study by Genovese (1974, pp. 555-556), the custom of dressing up when going out on non-labour days (in particular, the sabbath and holidays) may represent a pattern—with deep roots in lifestyles that have characterized the poor, highly religious blacks, and other groups, over the centuries of their presence in the United States.

> The slaves surprised contemporaries by a combination of indifference toward their appearance during the week and concern with their appearance on Sundays and holidays. 'With a passion for dress, they frequently spend all they make on fine clothes; their appearance on the sabbath and on public days is anything but an index of their fortunes and comfort at home' (Genovese 1974, p. 555).

Aside from the costume that may be donned, dressing up for display in a public place would be for naught if the person never left his or her dressing room. And, as shown in our study, the elderly we observed were not often disappointed. We found that dressing up and getting out occurred significantly more often in association with the receipt of visits from members of extra-institutional primary groups (G=.50, n=53, p<.001) than with visits from inmate friends (G=.24, n=53, p<.01). Although the latter relationship was significant, it was much weaker than the relationship between external visitors and egress from the institutional setting.

Getting Out, Anomia, Life Satisfaction and Self-Image

As we have shown above, frequent visits from relatives and friends, and opportunities to journey outside their residential settings were clearly important to the health and welfare of these elderly people. The significance, for mental health, of opportunities to get out is made most explicit in its relationship to changes in sense of anomia, loneliness and life dissatisfaction, and self-image.

There were also significant reductions in the sense of loneliness, or increases in reported life satisfaction, in association with increasing opportunities to get out (G=.34, n=72, p<.01). Finally, there were significant (although slight) improvements in level of self-image with increasing opportunities to visit with members of primary groups outside the long-term care settings (G=.18, n=72, p<.05).

Summary

In this chapter, we showed that frequent interaction with family members and friends had important positive influences on the general welfare of these elderly black people during the first eight to twelve months following their forced migration from Griot House. As structural or regulatory forces in the pattterns of elderly responses to their new life situations, old Griot House friends living in common post-relocation homes, and extra-institutional members of primary groups were not equally influential in determining the variations in all of the behaviors considered.

Visits from Old Griot House friends were significantly more influential (than visits from extra-institutional primary groups) in determining high levels of self-perceived health, perception of the quality of food services, and ability to sleep in the new residential settings. We interpreted this to mean that self-perceived health, eating, and sleeping were behaviors intricately associated with the internal order of the world of inmates of long-term care institutions, with only remote significance to external others. Consequently, inmates were more likely to look to each other—rather than to outsiders—in assessing these kinds of behaviors and other aspects of the everyday life of the inmate world. Furthermore, the significant relationship between visits from old friends and self-perceived health, eating, and sleeping was interpreted as an indicator of the strong influences of inmate relationships. A near zero relationship existed between these same behaviors and visits with inmates from outsiders.

Next, we found that external visits were significantly associated with reported happiness, increased activity levels, dressing up, and getting out. None of these behaviors were significantly related to visits by inmate friends. These clear differences, between correlates of insider and outsider visits, help to further confirm our interpretation of the behavioral influences of the organizational differences between the everyday life of the elderly inmates and the everyday life of their significant others on the outside.

We can conclude that elderly insiders of long-term care institutions are primarily oriented to the range of highly structured, (relatively) low-activity programs designed for them by the gatekeepers of the inmate world. By contrast, outside primary groups are less constrained by gatekeepers, are more oriented and engaged, on a daily basis, in a wider range of interactions with different kinds of people and public places, and are less limited in the range of activities that can punctuate the sequences of events in their everyday lives. Perhaps it is because of these and other differences that elderly inmates look with apparently pleasurable excitement toward forthcoming visits from members of outside primary groups, and show significant decreases in feelings of anomia, along with an improved sense of life satisfaction and self-image, when those visits are consummated.

CHAPTER 10

Summary and Conclusions

In this study we focused on the incidence of transplantation shock, or signs of distress, following residential relocation among two groups of elderly black people. Each group was involuntarily removed from a home for the elderly to one of a variety of other kinds of homes in a large metropolis of the industrial, northeastern United States, during the year 1976. In addition to the incidence of post-relocation mortality, we studied a variety of changes in personality and social behavior, such as self-image, felt loneliness, and patterns of interaction with family and friends.

Conceptual Framework

In Part I, we studied the social, psychological, and physiological background characteristics of the elderly. We assumed that the patterns of post-relocation responses to stress would, in large part, be patterned on the basis of behaviors learned and reinforced through pre-relocation experiences in coping with stress. As such, we focused in detail on the social organization of everyday life in Griot House (the home of origin), in an effort to isolate hypothetically useful predictors of post-relocation coping behavior. Among the most important hypothetical predictors identified before the inception of the relocation process were (1) high economic status, (2) the assignment of marked importance to religious beliefs and practices, and (3) close relations with family and friends (maintained, for example, through frequent visits). High physical self-maintenance ability, mental status, and dispositions to interact with other people were also important factors that helped to distinguish elderly with high self-imagery, positive outlook on life, and low agitation before their relocation.

We expected the following relationships between pre- and post-relocation behavior:

1. High levels of pre-relocation mental status and physical self-maintenance ability would be highly associated with low levels of transplantation shock.
2. Low levels of pre-relocation alienation would be associated with low levels of transplantation shock.
3. Pre-relocation preferences for low social distance from whites, or an expressed willingness to live in close proximity with white people, would be associated with a low incidence of transplantation shock among those black elderly who were moved to predominantly white homes.
4. The higher the level of pre-location socioeconomic status, the fewer the signs of transplantation shock.
5. Sustained positive social relations through the relocation process, and a relatively consistent flow of visits from friends and relatives would be highly associated with low levels of transplantation shock.

Findings

Mortality Rates

We found a host of factors that were significantly related to biological survival and positive levels of psychological and social adjustment following relocation. As we have already shown in Chapter 6, high physical self-maintenance ability, high mental status, and positive dispositions to interaction (extroversion) were the three factors that significantly distinguished all survivors from nonsurvivors during the first four to five months following relocation.

We also found that 100 percent of the post-relocation deaths had occurred among women in the study. In our search for explanatory variables, we found that women who had died were significantly lower (than their surviving counterparts) in felt loneliness and life dissatisfaction, as well as low in physical self-maintenance, mental status, and disposition to social interaction.

Contrary to previous research, we did not find increased levels in mortality rates in either of the two groups studied during the first four months after relocation. There was a significant decrease in mortality rates when our study groups were compared to both their own pre-relocation rates and to their controls. However, we found no clear explanation for these decreases in mortality rates.[1]

Some Propositions

As we proposed earlier in our survey of the literature, people—who had known a history of uncertainty and life in a hostile socioeconomic environment, punctuated by periodic uprooting, changes in places of residence, along with tenuous access to resources for economic well-being—may, over time, develop a degree of resilience or immunity against the otherwise shocking effects of involuntary relocation. By contrast, it would be expected that similar degrees of tolerance for uncertainty would not be present in the character of persons who had known residential stability, over time, and who had a relatively high degree of social and economic security in their life situations.

Furthermore, persons—who have known and lived a personal history of uncertainty, transiency in residential patterns, and distrust of other people—may turn inward, and reduce externally-oriented motor behavior and psychosocial activity by, for example, decreased interaction with other people under conditions of crises. By both a reduction in overall levels of environmental manipulatory behavior and little or no expectation that their manipulatory behaviors would be of any consequence, a person could enter what could be called a behavioral psychosocial cocoon, characterized by sharply reduced motor behavior and cognitive-affective withdrawl of attention from external environmental events. This kind of adjustment is similar to what Hinkle (1974) calls "emotional insulation." As interpreted by Gersten, Langner and Eisenberg (1977), emotional insulation refers to the ability of a person to experience major life changes with few noticeable health effects. The effect of the behavioral psychosocial cocoon (or emotional insulation) is a reduced sensitivity to what would otherwise be the shocking effects of radical social change— that could occur under conditions of forced residential relocation.

On the other hand, persons who had primarily known and come to expect highly stable and predictable residential environments could be expected to experience severe distress under conditions of forced residential change. These propositions are consistent with recent research (discussed in Chapter 8) on the relations between the internal versus external loci of control of individual and social actions.

Given this conceptual framework, the black elderly in this study may have shown decreased mortality rates as a consequence of increased externality of locus of control within the critical periods during and immediately following their forced relocation. Those few persons, whose deaths defined the increased rate for the month immediately preceding relocation in Group II, could have had their mortalities explained, in part, by their greater perceived internal loci of control.

Unfortunately, we did not have the data to conduct a rigorous test of these hypotheses. However, if we assume that high religiosity is an indicator of high externality, then we can claim indirect support for this (Chapter 8) interpretation. Elders who were high in religiosity showed fewer signs of transplantation shock than the low religiosity elderly in this study.

Physical Self-maintenance and Mental Status

Our findings generally supported our hypothesis that persons high in physical self-maintenance ability and mental status would show significantly lower signs of transplantation shock. There were significantly fewer deaths, as well as higher levels of self-image and life satisfaction, among the elderly who were rated high in physical self-maintenance and mental status. These findings were consistent with our hypotheses, the literature, and were discussed in detail in Chapters 6 through 8.

Social Alienation and Social Distance

Pre-relocation analyses of the relationships between alienation and other factors yielded no consistent and significant results. There were weak relationships with felt loneliness, life dissatisfaction, and agitation. But the results were not sharp enough to warrant an expectation that the Srole Anomia Scale, our measure of social alienation, would be sufficiently discriminating. There were no "real," substantive differences between these elderly in levels of alienation that would help to explain signs of transplantation shock, or the absence thereof.

In our post-relocation analyses, the results were not markedly different. However, we did find a relationship between increased levels of anomia and increased feelings of loneliness and life dissatisfaction among low religiosity elderly.

Contrary to our expectations, low distance elderly (those who showed little or no preference for post-residential segregation from whites) did not adjust any better than high distance black elderly in predominantly white settings. High distance elderly faired as well as, and in some instances, better than the low distance elderly, because, as we reasoned in Chapter 7, they may have expected less positive change in quality of life as a consequence of moving to a racially mixed residential setting.

The Significance of Economic Status

In Chapter 5, we showed that elderly persons high in economic status were more likely to be selected for visiting by low status others than were their counterparts. Further, we showed in Chapters 3 and 5 that high economic status was more highly associated with high levels of life satisfaction and self-image than any other factors, except visits received from friends and elderly peers. These findings were interpreted to mean that, in the absence of therapeutic intervention in long-term care institutions, elderly people with low economic status, low self-images, and deep feelings of loneliness will have a higher likelihood of persisting in those conditions—because they will have a lower likelihood of being chosen as targets for friendly visits, and other kinds of social, psychological, and economic supports that make improvements in self-image and increased life satisfaction possible.

We found indirect support for this interpretation in our studies of post-relocation behavior. The post-relocation analyses showed that the higher the levels of self-perceived economic status, the higher the levels of self-image and life satisfaction. Further, we found that high levels of self-perceived economic status and self-image were directly associated with positive attitudes toward new residential settings. By contrast, our composite objective measure of social class explained none of the variation in post-relocation psychological and social behavior.

Family and Friends in the Mitigation of Transplantation Shock

Close relations between the elderly, their offspring, other family members, and friends were significant throughout the study as factors that helped to explain high levels of self-image, sense of life satisfaction, low social alienation and felt agitation. These findings were discussed in detail in Chapters 3 through 5, and 7 through 9.

Conclusions

Our findings clearly showed that the residential relocation of elderly infirm persons was, in no sense, straightforward in the effects that it could produce. There was a variety of intervening variables that could significantly alter or inhibit (what might otherwise be) the serious, deleterious effects of involuntary relocation.

High religiosity, high self-perceived economic status, high physical self-maintenance ability, high mental status, positive disposition to social interaction, and sustained solidary relations with family and friends were significant determinants of positive adjustment to forced residential relocation. Further research is needed to determine more precisely the differential significance of these variables.

A Note on Policy Implications

The ability of administrators to formulate careful and comprehensive strategies for the relocation of poor, mentally-impaired elderly persons depends largely on the accuracy of the information available to them. Those plans that effect large groups of institutionalized elderly people, who have no choice in the decision to relocate, were especially germane to our study. For example, it is important for planners and administrators to be able to identify relocation procedures conducive to low levels of post-relocation mortality and other signs of transplantation shock. A growing volume of research findings, including our own, has begun to make this kind of planning possible. But, there are still many unanswered questions.

Supportive Groups in the Relocation of Elderly Infirm People

One of the major policy aims of research in this area is the need to identify techniques and strategies of intervention to reduce the stressful effects of relocation. Given our agreement with the importance of this objective, the work of the Pennsylvania State Relocation Team at Griot House was observed in its procedures for preparing the targeted elderly for relocation during the period of this study.

The relocation team focused on reducing anxieties and sustaining optimum levels of morale among the elderly, by helping them to think through relocation and prepare for a new home. As observers, we thought it was reasonable to expect (assuming that the team effort succeeded and that its effects could be partialed out) relatively high levels of morale for groups exposed to the team before actual relocation—in contrast to groups that were moved or relocated without prior exposure to the team. We found that participation of the relocation team was logistically helpful in the relocation of the elderly poor and infirm. However, there was no evidence that the relocation team was any more effective in reducing the signs of transplantation shock than family and friends of the elderly of Griot House, and the professional staff of the home. Our interpretations of these results appear in Chapters 5 through 7, and 9.

We recommend that future relocation projects should be more carefully planned to take into account the following factors:

1. Elderly preferences for social distance from ethnically divergent others: Where the elderly from a predominantly black or white home are being moved to a new home, that is largely or entirely opposite the home of origin in racial characteristics, careful planning and time should be given to preparing the elderly members, administrators, and staff of each home for the coming interaction, and identifiable differences in ethnic group customs that each should be prepared to adjust to. In so far as there are marked preferences for distance—or (conversely) living in a racially or ethnically homogeneous setting—every effort should be made to match pre- and post-relocation ethnic group characteristics of the residential settings.

2. In states where specialized teams are needed in the relocation of elderly disabled persons, special efforts should be made to build those teams from existing social service and/or nursing departments of the target homes. Relocation teams should not be composed solely of bureaucratic specialists who have no familiarity with the personalities and lifestyles of the elderly targeted for relocation.

3. Ideally, the agents of intervention should be the offspring, other family members, aged peers, or friendly visitors—who are deeply sensitive and familiar with the life situations of the elderly. Our evidence clearly shows the positive influences of these kinds of groups in the reduction of transplantation shock. Visiting behavior by relatives and friends was especially important, independent of the work of the state relocation team.

Note

1. Because of a work slowdown or "job action" of the Union of Computer Center Workers at Temple University that began in July, 1977, which developed into a full work stoppage in August, we could not get any electronic processing of data stored on tapes at the Computer Center after July 10, 1977. As a consequence, some of the phase three quantitative analyses of data that we had planned could not be completed at Temple University within the time limits of the grant period for this project. However, the data are on cards and further analyses are planned at the National Center on Black Aged, where I will take up residency as research director starting in the fall of 1977.

BIBLIOGRAPHY

Aguilera, Donna C. "Relationship between Physical Contact and Verbal Interaction between Nurses and Patients." *Journal of Psychiatric Nursing* (January-February 1967):13-17.

Aptheker, Herbert. *Annotated Bibliography of the Published Writings of W.E.B. DuBois,* New York: Kraus-Thomson Organization Limited, 1973.

Arth, M. "Ideals and Behavior: A Comment on Ibo Respect Patterns." *The Gerontologist* 8,4 (1968): 242-244.

Atchley, Robert C. *The Social Forces in Later Life.* Belmont, California: Wadsworth Publishing, 1977.

Atlanta University. *Atlanta University Publications,* Nos. 1-18, 1896-1914. New York: Arno Pess and the New York Times, 1968.

Bart, Pauline B. "Depression in Middle-Aged Women: Some Sociocultural Factors." Paper presented at the Annual Meeting of the Society for the Study of Social Problems, 1968. Boston, Massachusetts.

Billingsley, Andrew. *Black Families in White America.* Englewood Cliffs, New Jersey: Prentice-Hall, 1968.

Blackwell, James R. *The Black Community: Diversity and Unity.* New York: Dodd, Mead, 1975.

Blalock, Hubert M. *Causal Inferences in Non-experimental Research.* Chapel Hill: University of North Carolina Press, 1964.

Blenkner, M. "Environmental Change and The Aging Individual." *The Gerontologist* 7 (1967): 101-105.

Bogardus, Emory S. "A Social Distance Scale." *Sociology and Social Research* 17,3 (January-February 1974): 265-271.

Boggs, James. *The American Revolution.* New York: Monthly Review, 1965.

Boulware, Marcus Hanna. *The Oratory of Negro Leaders: 1900-1968.* Westpoint, Connecticut: Negro Universities Press, 1969.

Bourestom, Norman, and Tars, Sandra. "Alternations in Life Patterns Following Nursing Home Relocation." *The Gerontologist* 14,6 (December 1974).

Brody, Elaine M.; Kleban, Morton H.; Lawton, M. Powell; and Silverman, Herbert. "Excess Disabilities of Mentally Impaired Aged: Impact of Individualized Treatment." *The Gerontologist,* Part I (Summer 1971): 124-133.

Cayton, Horace R. "The Psychology of the Negro under Discrimination." In *Minority Problems.* Edited by Arnold M. Rose and Caroline B. Rose. New York: Harper and Row, 1965.

Chapin, F. Stuart. "The Effects of Slum Clearance and Rehousing on Family and Community Relationships in Minneapolis." *American Journal of Sociology* 43 (1933): 744-763.

Cooley, Charles H. *Social Organization: A Study of the Larger Mind.* New York: Schocken Books, 1962.

Cronbach, Lee J. *Essentials of Psychological Testing.* New York: Harper and Brothers, 1960.

Dancey, Joseph Jr. *The Black Elderly: A Guide for Practitioners.* Michigan: The Institute of Gerontology, University of Michigan—Wayne State University, 1977.

Dohrenwend, Barbara Snell, and Dohrenwend, Bruce, eds. *Stressful Life Events: Their Nature and Effects.* New York: John Wiley and Sons, 1974.

Drake, St. Clair, and Cayton, Horace. *Black Metropolis: A Study of Negro Life in a Northern City.* New York: Harper and Row, 1962.

DuBois, W.E.B. *Black Reconstruction in America, 1860-1880.* (1935) New York: Antheneum, 1969.

DuBois, W.E.B. "The Economics of Negro Emancipation." *The Sociological Review* (October 1911): 303-313.

DuBois, W.E.B. *The Philadelphia Negro.* Philadelphia: University of Pennsylvania Press, 1973.

DuBois, W.E.B. "The Shape of Fear." *North American Review* LLXXIII (June 1926): 291-304.

Dudley, Donald L., and Welke, Elton. *How to Survive Being Alive: Stress Points and Your Health.* New York: Doubleday, 1977.

Dunphy, Dexter C. *The Primary Group: A Handbook for Analysis and Field Research.* New York: Appleton-Century-Crots, 1972.

Durkheim, Emile. *Elementary Forms of the Religious Life.* New York: Macmillan, 1915.

Durkheim, Emile. "On the Learning of Discipline." In *Moral Education.* Paris: Felix Alcan, 1925: 147-149, 151-164. Reprinted in Parsons, Talcott, and Shils, Edward A. *Theories of Society.* Vol. 2. New York: The Free Press, 1961: 860-865.

Durkheim, Emile. *Suicide: A Study in Sociology.* Translated by John A. Spaulding and George Simpson. New York: The Free Press, 1951.

Eisdorfer, Carl. "Stress, Disease and Cognitive Change in the Aged." In *Cognitive and Emotional Disturbance in the Elderly.* Edited by Carl Eisdorfer and Robert O. Friedel. Chicago: Year Book Medical Publishers, 1977.

Faris, Robert E.L., and Dunham, Warren H. *Mental Disorders in Urban Areas: An Ecological Study of Schizophrenia and Other Psychoses.* Chicago: The University of Chicago Press, 1967.

Fauset, Arthur Huff. *Black Gods of the Metropolis: Negro Religious Cults in the Urban North.* Philadelphia: University of Pennsylvania Press, 1971.

Fisher, Walter. "Physicians and Slavery in the Antebellum Southern Medical Journal." In *The Making of Black America. Volume I. The Origins of Black Americans.* Edited by August Meier and Elliot Rudwick, New York: Atheneum, 1969.

Foucault, Michel. *Madness and Civilization: A History of Insanity in the Age of Reason.* New York: The New American Library, 1965.

Frazier, Franklin E. "Desegregation as an Object of Sociological Study." In *Human Behavior and Social Process.* Edited by Arnold M. Rose. Boston: Houghton Mifflin, 1962: 608-624.

Frazier, Franklin E. *The Negro Church in America.* New York: Schocken Books, 1963.

Frazier, Franklin E. *The Negro Family in the United States.* Chicago: The University of Chicago Press, 1966.

Frazier, Franklin E. *The Negro in the United States.* New York: MacMillan, 1957.

Freeman, Linton C. *Elementary Applied Statistics.* New York: John Wiley and Sons, Inc., 1965.

Fried, Marc. "Grieving for a Lost Home." In *The Urban Condition.* Edited by Leonard Duhl. New York: Basic Books, 1963.

Friedman, M., and Rosenman, R.H. "Association of Specific Overt Behavior Pattern with Blood and Cardiovascular Findings: Blood Clotting Time, Incidence of Arcus Senilis and Clinical Artery Disease." *Journal of the American Medical Association* 169 (1959): 1286-1296.

Fromm, Eric. *The Art of Loving.* London: Unwin, 1962.

Gans, Herbert. "Planning for Urban Renewal." *Transaction* 1,1 (November 1963): 5-17, 19.

Garvin, Richard M., and Burger, Robert E. *Where They Go to Die.* New York: Delcorte Press, 1968.

Genovese, Eugene F. *Roll, Jordan, Roll: The World the Slaves Made.* New York: Pantheon Books, 1974.

Gersten, Joanne C.; Langner, Thomas S.; Eisenberg, Jeanne G.; and Fagan-Simacha, Ora. "An Evaluation of the Etiologic Role of Stressful Life-Change Events in Psychological Disorders." *Journal of Health and Social Behavior* 18,3 (September 1977): 228-244.

Gibbs, Jack P. "Suicide." In *Contemporary Social Problems*. Edited by R. Merton and R.S. Nisbet. New York: Harcourt, Brace and World, 1972.

Glass, David C. *Behavior Patterns, Stress, and Coronary Disease*. Hillsdale, New Jersey: Lawrence Erlbaum Associates, 1977.

Goffman, Erving. *Asylums*. New York: Doubleday, 1961.

Goffman, Erving. *Behavior in Public Places*. New York: The Free Press, 1963a.

Goffman, Erving. *Stigma: Notes on the Management of Spoiled Identity*. Englewood Cliffs, New Jersey: Prentice-Hall, 1963b.

Gore, P.M., and Rotter, Julian B. "A Personality Correlate of Social Action." *Journal of Personality* 31 (1963): 58-64.

Haley, Alex. *Roots: The Saga of an American Family*. New York: Doubleday, 1976.

Ham, Joseph Neal. "The Forgotten Minority: An Exploration of Long Term Institutionalized Aged and Aging Male Prison Inmates." Ph.D Dissertation. The University of Michigan (Microfilms), Ann Arbor, Michigan: 1976.

Handlin, Oscar. *The Uprooted*. Boston: Little, Brown, 1973.

Hartman, Chester. "Social Values, and Housing Orientations." *Journal of Social Issues* (April 1963): 113-131.

Hill, Robert. *The Strengths of Black Families*. New York: Emerson Hall Press, 1972.

Hinkle, L.E. Jr. "The Effect of Exposure to Culture Change, Social Change, and Changes in Interpersonal Relationships on Health." In *Stressful Life Events: Their Nature and Effects*. Edited by Barbara Snell Dohrenwend, and Bruce P. Dohrenwend. New York: John Wiley and Sons, 1974.

Hollingshead, August B., and Redlich, Frederick C. *Social Class and Mental Illness: A Community Study*. New York: John Wiley and Sons, 1958.

Hollinghead, August B., and Redlich, Frederick C. "Social Stratification and Psychiatric Disorders." *American Sociological Review* 18 (April 1953): 164-169.

Hull, Richard W. *Munyakare: African Civilization Before the Batuuree*. New York: John Wiley and Sons, 1972.

Institute of Gerontology. *Death and Survival: Relocation Report Number 2*. Ann Arbor Michigan: University of Michigan—Wayne State University, 1975.

Jackson, Jacqueline Johnson. "Social Stratification of Aged Blacks and Implications for Training Professionals." In *Proceedings of Black Aged in the Future*. Edited by J.J. Jackson, Washington, D.C.: The National Caucus on the Black Aged, Inc., and The Gerontological Society, 1972.

Jourard, Sidney. *Disclosing Man to Himself*. New York: Reinhold, 1968.

Kirkpatrick, Clifford. *The Family: As Process and Institution*. New York: The Ronald Press, 1963.

Langner, T.S., and Michael, S.T. *Life, Stress, and Mental Health*. New York: Free Press, 1963.

Lauer, Robert H., and Warren H. Handel *Social Psychology: The Theory And Application of Symbolic Interaction*. Boston, Houghton Mifflin, 1977.

Lawton, M. Powell. "Morale: What Are We Measuring?" Paper presented at the meetings of the Gerontological Society. Louisville: November 1975a.

Lawton, M. Powell. "The Philadelphia Geriatric Center Morale Scale: A Revision." *Journal of Gerontology* 30,1 (1975b): 85-89.

Lawton, M. Powell, and Yaffe, Sylvia. "Mortality, Morbidity and Voluntary Change of Residence by Older People." *Journal of American Geriatrics Society* 18,10 (1970): 823-831.

Lenski, Gerhard. *The Religious Factor*. New York: Doubleday, 1963.

Lieberman, Morton A. "Relationship of Mortality Rates to Entrance to a Home for the Aged." *Geriatrics*. 16,10 (October 1961): 515-519.

Logan, Rayford W. *The Negro in the United States*. Princeton, New Jersey: D. Van Nostrand, 1957.

Lowenthal, Marjorie Fisk. *Lives in Distress*. New York: Basic Books, 1964.

Lowenthal, Marjorie Fisk. "Psychosocial Variations Across the Adult Life Course: Frontiers for Research and Policy." *The Gerontologist* 15,6 (1975).

Marlowe, Roberta A. "Effects of Relocating Geriatric State Hospital Patients." Paper presented at the 25th annual meetings of The Gerontological Society. San Juan, Puerto Rico: December 1972.

Marx, Karl. "Contribution to the Critique of Hegel's Philosophy of Right." In *Karl Marx: Early Writings*. Edited by T.B. Bottomore. New York: McGraw Hill Books, 1964.

Mauss, Marcel. *The Gift: Forms and Function of Exchange in Archaic Societies*. New York: W.W. Norton, 1967.

Mays, Benjamin Elijah, and Nicholson, Joseph Williams. *The Negro's Church*. New York: 1933.

Miller, David, and Lieberman, Morton A. "The Relationship of Affect State and Adaptive Capacity to Reactions to Stress." *Journal of Gerontology* 20,4 (October 1965): 492-497.

Morris, Charles. *Sigmification and Significance*. Cambridge, Massachussetts: The M.I.T. Press, 1964.

Myrdal, Gunnar. *An American Dilemma*. New York: Harper and Brothers, 1944.

Nobles, Wade W. "Africanity: Its Role in Black Families." *The Black Scholar* 5,9 (June 1974): 10-17.

O'Hara, John D. "Status Quo at the Stephen Smith Home for the Aged—as per Meeting of April of April 8, 1976." Commonwealth of Pennsylvania: April 9, 1976.

Parsons, Talcott. "Age and Sex in the Social Structure of the United States." In *Essays in Sociological Theory*. Edited by Talcott Parsons. New York: The Free Press, 1954.

Pastalan, Leon. "Pennsylvania Nursing Home Relocation Program/Interim Research Findings." Ann Arbor, Michigan: Institute of Gerontology, University of Michigan—Wayne State University, 1976.

Riley, M.W.; Johnson, M.E.; and Foner, A. *Aging and Society: A Sociology of Age Stratification*. New York: Russell Sage Foundation, 1971.

Rogers, Carl. *On Becoming a Person.* Boston: Houghton Mifflin Company, 1961.

Roscow, Irving. "The Social Effects of the Physical Environment." *H.A.I.P.* 27,2 (May 1961): 127-133.

Rose, Arnold M. "Inconsistencies in Attitudes Toward Negro Housing." In *Minority Problems.* Edited by Arnold M. and Caroline B. Rose. New York: Harper and Row, 1965.

Rose, Arnold M. "Race Relations in Housing." *Social Problems* 12 (1964): 245-247.

Rotter, Julian B. "Generalized Expectancies for Internal Versus External Control of Reinforcement." *Psychological Monographs* 80 (1966): Whole Number 609.

Rotter, Julian B. "Level of Aspiration as a Method of Studying Personality, II. Group Validity Studies." *Character and Personality* 11 (1943): 254-274.

Rubenstein, Daniel I. "An Examination of Social Participation Found Among a National Sample of Black and White Elderly." Paper read at the Eastern Psychological Association Annual Meeting, 1971.

Rumney, Jay, and Shuman, S. *The Social Effects of Public Housing.* Newark, New Jersey: Newark Housing Authority, 1944.

Sainsbury, Peter. *Suicide in London: An Ecological Study.* New York: Basic Books, 1956.

Sampson, Edward A. *Social Psychology and Contemporary Society.* New York: John Wiley, 1971.

Selye, Hans. *The Stress of Life.* New York: McGraw-Hill Books, 1976.

Sherwood, Sylvia; Morris, John N.; and Barnhart, Esther. "Developing a System for Assigning Individuals into an Appropriate Residential Setting." *Journal of Gerontology* 30,3 (1975): 331-342.

Shils, Edward. "The Study of the Primary Group." In *The Policy Sciences.* Edited by Daniel Lerner and Harold Lasswell. Stanford, California: Stanford University Press, 1951.

Sigerist, Henry E. *Civilization and Disease.* Chicago: The University of Chicago Press, 1943.

Srole, Leo. "Social Integration and Certain Corollaries: An Exploratory Study." *American Sociological Review* 21,6 (December 1956): 709-716.

Stanton, A.H., and Schwartz, M.S. *The Mental Hospital.* New York: Basic Books, 1954.

Staples, Robert. "The Black Family in Evolutionary Perspective." *The Black Scholar* 5,9 (June 1974): 2-9.

Storandt, Martha; Wittels, Illene; and Botwinick, Jack. "Predictors of a Dimension of Well-Being in the Relocated Healthy Aged." *Journal of Gerontology* 30,1 (1975): 97-102.

Stotsky, Bernard A. *The Elderly Patient.* New York: Grune and Straton, 1968.

Sussman, Marvin B., ed. *Sociology and Rehabilitation.* Washington, D.C.: American Sociological Association, 1966.

Townsend, Peter, *The Last Refuge*. London: Rutledge and Kegan Paul, 1964.

Watson, Wilbur H. "Aging and Race." *Social Action* 38,3 (November 1971): 20-30.

Watson, Wilbur H. "The Aging Sick and the Near Dead: A Study of Some Distinguishing Characteristics and Social Effects." *Omega—The Journal of Death and Dying* 11,2 (Summer 1976): 115-123.

Watson, Wilbur H. "Body Idiom in Social Interaction: A Field Study of Geriatric Nursing." Doctoral Dissertation. Department of Sociology, University of Pennsylvania (Van Pelt Library), Philadelphia, Pennsylvania: 1972.

Watson, Wilbur H. "The Meanings of Touch: Geriatric Nursing." *Journal of Communications* 25,3 (Summer 1975): 104-112.

Watson, Wilbur H. "Patterns of Family Response to a Mentally Retarded Child: A Study of a Black Family." In *Disabled Families*. Edited by Samuel Z. Klausner. Philadelphia: University of Pennsylvania and the Center for Research on the Acts of Man, 1969.

Watson, Wilbur H. "Self-Evaluation and Evaluation of Marital Adjustment." Master's Thesis. Kent State University Library, Kent, Ohio: 1966.

Watson, Wilbur H. *Sustaining the Black Elderly in Their Homes in an Urban Area: The Impact of the Stephen Smith Centers for Older Adults*. Philadelphia, Pennsylvania: The Stephen Geriatric Center, 1978.

Watson, Wilbur H., and Maxwell, Robert J. *Human Aging and Dying: A Study in Socio-Cultural Gerontology*. New York: Saint Martins Press, 1977.

Wax, Rosalie H., and Thomas, Robert K. "American Indians and White People." *Phylon* 22,4 (Winter 1961): 305-317.

Weber, Max. *From Max Weber: Essays in Sociology*. New York: Oxford University Press, 1947.

Wright, Beatrice A. *Physical Disability: A Psychological Approach*. New York: Harper and Row, 1960.

Wylie, Floyd M. "Attitudes Toward Aging and the Aged Among Black Americans: Some Historical Perspectives." *Aging and Human Development* 2 (1971): 66-70.

Yawney, Beverly A., and Slover, Darrel L. "Relocation of the Elderly." *Social Work* 18 (May 1973): 88-95.

INDEX

African attitude: classic, 3

Aging: in relation to church attendance, 47; attitudes toward own, 51-52

Agitation: in relation to morale, 51; and marital status, 50-51; and church attendance, 45-48

Alienation: socially defined, 45; in relation to loner behavior in church activity, 46

Andrus Foundation: in relation to the NRTA-AARP, xi

Anomia: defined, 45

Attitude toward own age: definition of, 47; influence of visits from children, 54

Church: affiliations, 37; determinants of participation, 38-47; activity in relation to physical and mental status, 38-40; going to meetings alone and in groups, 42-48; church going as an individual activity, 42; in relation to aging and male/female attendance, 47

Cocoon, psychosocial, 111; as a response to stress, 111; as signified by introversion, 74, 94

Death: as a relocation effect, 63-68, 82; in relation to stress among older black women, 68-70; rates among persons relocated by bureaucrats versus family and friends, 73-75.

Distress, vi; as a relocation effect, 63-64

Dressing up: in association with visiting behavior, 105-06

Durkheim, Emile: theory of social solidarity and intermediate groups, 3, 11, 47; extension to analyzing the stress reducing effect of friendship ties during crises, 73-74

Eating behavior: and the receipt of post relocation visits, 103-04

Economic status, 20-22; in relation to family assistance in the relocation of an elderly member, 21-22; self-perceived, 91-93; in relation to perceived improvements in post-relocation housing, 93

Elderly: Ibo of West Africa, 2; Chinese, 2; traditional respect for black American, 2

Emotional insulation, 111; as a response to radical social change, 111

Ethnicity: in relation to matching pre- and post-relocation settings of migratory elderly persons, 79-86

Extroversion, 55-57; as a determinant of physically surviving forced residential change, 74

Family: in relation to the older institutionalized person, 52-54; as agents in the relocation of elderly members, 53; and post-relocation visiting behavior, 101-08

125